DISCARD

And
Never Stop
Dancing

Also by Gordon Livingston

Too Soon Old, Too Late Smart

Only Spring

And Never Stop Dancing

*Thirty More True Things
You Need to Know Now*

Gordon Livingston, M.D.

MARLOWE & COMPANY
NEW YORK

For my children
Kirsten, Nina, Andrew, Michael, Emily, and Lucas
Though much is taken, much abides.

And grandchildren
Tatiana, Karl, and Felipe
Our gifts to the 21st century

After a bomb killed two dozen young people at a Tel Aviv disco a few years ago, Israeli youth refused to be cowed. They resumed a robust nightlife. Today, outside the scene of the bombing, beneath a stone memorial listing the names of the dead, is a single inscription: LO NAFSEEK LIRKOD. *It means, "We won't stop dancing."*

—Gene Weingarten, *The Washington Post Magazine*

Contents

Acknowledgments

M any people's ideas are contained in this book. My failure to acknowledge them individually is not ingratitude; there are so many that I know that in doing so, I would inevitably omit someone whose thoughts I have borrowed.

But I must here pay tribute to my exceptional editor and publisher, Matthew Lore. For his friendship, unstinting support, sharp editorial eye, and willingness to believe in this book and its predecessors, I will always be grateful; few writers can have been so fortunate. And to my agent, the estimable Rafe Sagalyn, who in a time of great personal trial still managed to act on my behalf. I am also indebted to Jim Finefrock, editor of the Insight section of the *San Francisco Chronicle*, and to Richard Gross, op-ed page editor of the *Baltimore Sun*; both have generously allowed my voice to be heard on issues important to me. Thanks to my friend and colleague Tom Ferguson, who saw possibilities in my search for useful truths and was the first to encourage me to write them down. To my daughter Emily, herself a gifted writer, who offered crucial suggestions on the manuscript and continues to inspire me with her passion, values, and tolerance for all my mistakes as a parent. Finally, my wife, Clare, embodies everything that I admire and, after thirty-two years, surprises me daily with her willingness to share my life.

Paradox governs our lives.

In thirty-six years of listening to patients talk about their dreams and discontents, it has become apparent to me that most of us have a lot of difficulty figuring out what it means to be happy and how to achieve and sustain this desirable state.

One would think that, living in the most affluent society the world has ever seen at a time in which our material welfare is virtually guaranteed, where our natural enemies have been subdued and most of the infectious diseases that threatened human life contained, we might have the leisure to figure out ways of living and relating to each other that would produce sustained feelings of fulfillment and contentment. That this is not the case is what keeps people like me in business.

What, exactly, is our problem? What is it about the human condition that stands between us and the lives we desire?

As someone who works with his head and heart, I always admired those who work with their hands. I spent a lot of time on a farm when I was young and became adept at, among other things, converting dead trees into firewood. Some years ago, when I bought a house in the suburbs, I installed a woodstove and started scavenging for fuel. One day I passed a house with a dead oak tree in the front yard and stopped to ask the homeowner if I could take it down in exchange for the wood. He seemed happy for me to do so.

I dropped it into the street and over the course of a day converted it into a large stack of firewood. As I hauled the last of it away, the homeowner expressed his gratitude and told me that a tree company had wanted to charge him $500 for this service. I decided to go into business. I discovered that to become a "licensed tree expert" one had to take a written and practical exam. I showed up in my state capital on the appointed day and found myself in a room with a lot of young guys wearing flannel shirts and three-day beards.

The written test was easy enough, but then we had to accompany an examiner on a stroll through the streets of town. He would point out a tree and we had to write down its species name on an answer sheet. It was the middle of winter, so while those who knew their trees better than I did wrote their answers down, I was on my hands and knees trying to scare up some recognizable leaves.

In any event, I got the license, put an ad in the paper, and, over the next couple of years, cut down a lot of trees. It seemed to me a more productive way to exercise than running on a treadmill at the local sports club. Then I paid a real tree expert to teach me to climb, which added to the charm of the experience, though it did create some homeowner consternation when, as frequently happened, my on-call beeper went off and I had to climb down the tree to use their phone to talk to the hospital emergency room.

Anyway, climbing and cutting trees usually drew a crowd of interested onlookers. One day when I was going up a dead hickory, I grabbed a branch that broke off in my hand and I fell about thirty feet onto a lawn, narrowly missing a flagstone walk and a couple of spectators. As I lay there stunned and embarrassed, a man rushed up and began palpating my thyroid gland while reassuring me, "Don't worry, I'm a doctor." So I said, "What kind of doctor are you?" "I'm a dermatologist," he answered. In the distance I could hear the siren of the approaching ambulance. Shortly after my broken back healed, I folded the tree business.

I tell this story because, like so much of life, it contains plenty of both good and bad news: My dreams of earning bread from the sweat of my brow were realized, but my health suffered. To swing gracefully from your climbing rope requires that you first get up the tree. People admire those who take physical risks, but it's also entertaining when they plunge to the ground. I have plenty of firewood, but my bad back makes it difficult to carry it into the house. And so on.

I have come to believe that an important force in people's lives might be called the determinative role of paradox. Sometimes when something happens to us it is many years before we know whether it was fortunate or disastrous. Many of our favorite folk sayings are expressions of this truth: "Too much of a good thing is bad." "He who wants everything, risks everything." "God punishes us by answering our prayers." We succeed in our work at the expense of our families. The love of our youth is the bane of our middle age. Experience makes us wiser but time defeats us. The more things change, the more they remain the same.

It is the discovery that "obeying the rules" does not always, or perhaps even usually, lead to fulfillment that is the biggest disillusionment of all. It turns out that many of the rules we follow were constructed to protect the interests and privileges of someone other than us. This is why so many people feel themselves in the grip of influences they cannot control: faceless bureaucracies, large corporations, economic forces—all the engines of a society that guarantees the pursuit of happiness but sets many obstacles on the path to its achievement.

In an effort to describe what constitutes acceptable behavior, it falls to the institutions of mental health to play their roles in defining "normality." Psychiatry has done its part by constructing the *Diagnostic and Statistical Manual of Mental Disorders*, now in its fourth edition. Within this weighty compendium are descriptions of various forms of behavior deemed abnormal by this society. Here we have the major mental illnesses—schizophrenia, bipolar disorder, major depression—alongside all the forms of anxiety and discouragement that cause people to seek help. Included as well are those maladaptive and troublesome patterns of behavior that comprise the "personality disorders": antisocial, compulsive, dependent, avoidant—all the people who annoy, exploit, and alienate their fellow citizens.

We appear to have a genetic loading for a variety of attributes. Identical twins raised apart have a high likelihood of suffering similar mental disorders. There is also evidence of a high concordance for personality characteristics, notably antisocial personality disorder. In the struggle between nature and nurture, both, not surprisingly, turn out to be important in determining the kinds of people we are.

Amid all this diagnosing and describing of human behavior, we are still confronted with the essential questions of how to live, how to discern what it is that we are responsible for, and what we must accommodate. One analogy is to heart disease. Clearly there are things that predispose us to suffer coronary events over which we have no control—our gender and genetic backgrounds, for example. If you are a man whose family history is one of early death from heart attacks in its male members, it is a good idea to refrain from smoking, watch your diet, and exercise regularly. But you still stand a good chance of suffering a myocardial infarction. So does it make sense to say "the hell with it" and eat, drink, and smoke as you please for as long as you can? That, of course, is a personal decision.

One author has defined happiness as a ratio between accomplishment and expectations. If the numerator of that fraction is sufficiently large—if we have done enough with our lives, however we define that—we have a good chance of being happy. If, however, the denominator, expectations, are sufficiently great, they can overcome whatever we have accomplished and we are left feeling unfulfilled. What is important to notice is that, insofar as the subjective experience of happiness is concerned, both components of the ratio are *self-defined.* What, to each of us, represents a satisfying level of accomplishment? And how does this match up with the expectations we have of ourselves? This concept usefully explains why people we might consider less fortunate materially than we are might be living happier lives and is the source of the truism that money can't buy happiness. (Though it must be said that Malcolm Forbes maintained that anyone who believed this was shopping in the wrong places.)

The best strategy for living, then, seems to be to control what we can without indulging the illusion that we can control everything. Perhaps another way of expressing this is through yet another paradox: *We gain maximum control when we relinquish the fantasy of total control.* Again we are attempting to walk a line between the extremes of helplessness and omnipotence.

If this sounds like a plea for moderation, perhaps it is. I prefer to think of it this way: If we are to be happy in a world where bad things happen routinely and unexpectedly, we need to keep our expectations realistic and develop a resilience to tragedy that will protect us from despair. We need to attune ourselves to the good news/bad news paradox and develop a capacity for accepting what we must. We also need to learn the art of letting go: of the past, of unresolved grievances, of our younger selves. Nobody gets out of here alive. Whether this reality is a reason for despair or an incentive to mobilize the courage required to get up each morning is a matter of attitude. This is where we have a choice.

*Much of what we think
we know is untrue.*

We all have our blind spots—things about the world or about ourselves that we firmly believe, even when the evidence suggests otherwise. In my experience as a psychiatrist, most people have a modest opinion of themselves in most respects. (Of course, I see more than my share of depressed people.) It's true that if you ask almost anyone how old they feel, they will subtract ten years from their chronological age, but very few people are delusional about it. We know how old we really are. If we refuse to acknowledge it to others, we also know we're lying.

Not many adults believe that they're extremely attractive, exactly the right weight, superintelligent, or destined for greatness. There is even a handy adjective, courtesy of Freud, for those who think too highly of themselves: narcissistic. (Though I am mindful of the traditional caution that "a narcissist is anyone better-looking than you are.")

With the notable exception of those we pay to entertain us, most people tend to underestimate their strengths. Consider, then, your answers to the following questions: Are you an insightful person? Do you have a good sense of humor? Are you a good driver? Try these on friends and family and note the small number who say no. Some of the least introspective people I encounter credit themselves with a great capacity for self-understanding. And don't try to talk them out of it. I hear various explanations for all forms of emotional distress, but seldom does someone say, "I think my problem is imbedded in my personality, but I've never really looked below the surface of my life; I'm just on autopilot." Sometimes I can talk people into considering such things as unconscious motives or maladaptive thinking. Sometimes not.

The ability to laugh (especially at ourselves) is a valuable defense mechanism and one of the most effective antidotes to life's plentiful tragedies. There was a time when, confronted by patients I was seeing in therapy who said they had a good sense of humor, I asked them to tell me a joke. This is obviously unfair and not a true test of anything except memory. Now, I just give people punch lines to famous stories and ask them to re-create the lead-in. Try it:

"If the fourth one quits, we'll be up here all day."

"The captain wants to go water-skiing in the morning."

"I forgot to call you yesterday."

"Just be out of the house when I get home."

Fun, isn't it? Not for everybody. If you are zero for four, go to GordonLivingston.com and click on "jokes." (This is a game for humor experts. Please do not risk your closest relationships by trying it at home.)

As for driving, little needs to be said. People sit in front of me with histories of speeding citations, multiple accidents, incarceration for DWI. All are certain that they are skillful drivers, subject to the vagaries of luck or overzealous law enforcement. Who among us can motor down the highway and not be puzzled by the certain knowledge that the woman driving next to us putting on lipstick and the man who just cut us off would, if asked, both classify themselves as excellent drivers?

Like the famous three lies ("The check is in the mail," "I love you," and "The flight will be delayed about an hour"), the three questions tell us something about ourselves and about the human condition. We may long to win the lottery or appear on national TV. What would really improve our lives is to laugh more, think about why we're here, and let each other merge.

Forgiveness is a gift we give ourselves.

For a time after the massacre in 1999, on a hill over-looking Columbine High School, stood fifteen crosses, memorials to both the victims and the perpetrators. Then the father and stepfather of one of the dead children removed the two crosses bearing the names of the shooters. They questioned the propriety of honoring murderers in the same place as their victims.

And so, while we were still struggling with the meaning, if any, of this tragedy, we were confronted with the question of what attitude we should take toward it. After the funerals and the ceremonies of remembrance, these events, like the sea of flowers placed near the school, began to fade. Our designated commentators turned elsewhere for opinion fodder, and the story of how two suburban boys chose to celebrate Hitler's birthday became a part of the river of events that flows by us and is lost to the memory of all but the families of the dead. Only the bereaved can understand what it is like to live in a world that does not notice their permanently unhealed wounds. If we are destined to forget, we might at least consider the possibility of forgiveness.

We are not a very forgiving nation. Much of our law, which is to say our principal attempt at justice, is based on the concept of retribution. The idea of getting even, when that is clearly not possible, is deeply imbedded in the culture. To cite only two examples: 74 percent of Americans favor the death penalty, and we live in the most litigious society in the world. No mistake involving injury to others, real or imagined, is tolerated. Victimization and blaming are national pastimes.

In this atmosphere, it is not surprising that forgiveness is unfashionable. One definition of the word is "giving up a grievance to which you are entitled." Widely confused with forgetting or reconciliation, it is neither. Forgiveness is an act of letting go, of relinquishment. It is not something we do for others; it is a gift to ourselves. The shooters at Columbine High inflicted the death penalty on themselves. What is left for us to do to them? We do not release them from accountability by forgiving; we free ourselves from the burden of bitterness. In this sense forgiveness is a selfish rather than an altruistic act.

People present themselves for psychotherapy burdened by grievances. Abusive childhoods, alcoholic parents, bad marriages—misfortunes of every type—are offered as "explanations" for one's current mood or behavior. The disadvantage of these formulations is that, though we have all been shaped to some extent by our past, none of us has the power to change what has happened. To relinquish the hold that the past has on us requires a conscious choice and, paradoxically, requires no strength, only courage. It necessarily involves forgiveness, not just of those who have hurt us, but also of ourselves, for the myriad mistakes, shortcomings, and wasted opportunities that mark our lives.

Through the medium of television, we have all been washed in the blood of innocents. The images of Colorado have been succeeded by those from Darfur and from Iraq. Are there sins past forgiving? I suppose so. Who can blame the father who took down the crosses of his daughter's murderers? But, in one sense, the whole massacre can be seen as a failure of forgiveness. For both these boys were reportedly mistreated and alienated, and cultivated an explosive hate in their hearts. No excuse can be offered for their crimes, but if we are truly to understand what happened (as we say we wish to), it cannot be with the same spirit that they brought to their ghastly work.

Forgiveness and justice are not incompatible goals. We can hold people accountable for their behavior without imagining that evil exists only outside ourselves or that life is as simple as we may have been led to believe.

In 2005, a twenty-six-year-old single mother, Ashley Smith, demonstrated an ability to simultaneously plead for her life and identify with the needs, emotional and spiritual, of Brian Nichols, the Atlanta courthouse shooter who had on that day already murdered four people. After spending several hours talking with her, he let her go and surrendered peacefully to police.

Giving Smith all the credit for her own survival overlooks the human interaction that occurred between these two very different people. Her decision to connect with him around family and religion clearly saved her life, while it revealed the complexity of the person she was dealing with. (Her own complexity became evident with her later revelation that she had shared with him her small stash of illegal drugs.) He was allegedly a rapist and certainly a murderer, yet he did not attack her. She became a person to him, deserving of life and respect. When he released her, she thought that he must have known that she would call the police.

If he is to retain the image of a monster without a conscience, then we must ignore the evidence of his humanity that his hostage used to survive. In keeping with the black/white (literally in this case) view of the world, he must be the repository of our fears of evil and violence, while she must be designated a hero, though she acted at all times in the way she calculated would give her the best chance of staying alive. She thought if she treated him like a human being and won his trust he might let her go, and he did.

Brian Nichols, it appears, was looking for something as he ran from the law, something that turned out to be more important even than his freedom. Over the course of that long night of conversation, he came to see the hand of the Almighty in his choosing to take this woman hostage. "He said that I was an angel sent from God. I was his sister and he was my brother in Christ." In fact, she was more like a good mother. She listened to him, argued against his taking his own life, offered him a kind of forgiveness, and cooked him a meal.

Our choice of heroes says a lot about us: firemen whose job it is to run into buildings that sometimes fall on them, soldiers who die randomly in combat, a Christian woman who saves herself using her intuition and religious beliefs.

How about this? Ashley Smith taught us all a valuable lesson about the power of faith and empathy and hoping for the best in desperate circumstances. Brian Nichols showed us that even the most violent among us are susceptible to kindness, humanity, and pancakes for breakfast.

Marriage ruins a lot of good relationships.

This is the tyranny of marriage: the vows which bind us allow us to become our worst selves. Thrown dishes, slammed doors, faces contorted like an infant's—all part of the contract. No one tells us this. No one tells us that the only unconditional love in this world is between parent and child. . . . But passion between a man and a woman is finite. If it lasts a thousand days, count yourself among the lucky . . .

There [is] no loneliness like marriage.

—Dani Shapiro, *Picturing the Wreck*

W hat are we looking for that draws us irresistibly toward marriage? There is, to be sure, the expectation that we grow up with, that we will find someone with whom we can form a pair-bond that has all sorts of practical advantages, from tax deductions to the division of labor that makes raising children easier. Marriage also, for many, represents an end to a prolonged search and a relief from the anxious, rejection-laden territory occupied by single people.

Whatever the advantages of being single—independence, flexibility, and the possibility of exciting sex with multiple partners—a glance at any of the very popular Internet dating sites suggests that practically everybody wants to be in a committed relationship.

When we finally decide to marry, everyone is happy for us. We step aboard the wedding express that bears us inexorably to the most grand (and expensive) day of our lives. I have had many people, usually in the throes of separation and divorce, speak of their misgivings as this day approached, all of which were swept aside by families intent on getting this passage over with. I hear again and again that "the invitations had been sent" or "the flowers had been paid for" as explanations for not listening to the still, small voice of doubt.

And so these uncertain brides and grooms go ahead, only

to discover in about half the cases that the person they married became, over time, someone else, someone they no longer loved. And what led them to this revelation? Infidelity, abusiveness, often simply boredom. "We grew apart," they say; "I found someone else"; "I can't stand the fighting any longer." And when I ask what they fought about, it's always the same: children, money, sex, in-laws, all the things that consume a marriage when partners don't love each other anymore. A failing marriage is like a bad meal: too little of what we want, too much of what we hate.

Then comes the bitter divorce, in which surrogates are hired to fight a legal battle that no one wins. Finally, the former lovers are divorced and are ready to start again the uncertain adventure of looking for a soul mate. The fact that not much is learned in this whole painful process is clear from the fact that second marriages have a higher failure rate than first marriages.

Why is it so hard to get it right? It might be the fault of our mothers. Either they loved us so much that no other adult can match them or they didn't love us enough so we're still children looking for that unconditional approval that few spouses are willing to provide. Maybe it's all a matter of unrealistic expectations. Hollywood might be to blame.

Many of us are seduced by the romantic idea that marriage represents: We have found the person who will complete us.

Since few among us feel complete, it's not surprising that we're looking for help. The trouble is that at the point in our young adulthoods when we're searching for someone to take on this ambitious task, we are still—how to put this delicately?—stupid. Or at least inexperienced in how the world works and what we can reasonably expect from other people. Mostly, we are suffering from a dearth of good information about how to tell the good guys from the bad guys, much less predict what either will be like in twenty years, even ten years, even five.

So we make mistakes. After listening to someone go on and on about what a terrible person his or her spouse turned out to be, I often say something like, "I guess he changed as a person in a way you would never have predicted." The response is usually, "Yes, that's exactly what happened." Then I say, "OK, that's called a mistake. One of the rules of life is that, in general, we have to pay for our mistakes. What you're feeling at the moment is your payment."

This line of conversation is not always well received. When one is complaining about someone else being at fault, it is uncomfortable to be reminded that this person was chosen as a spouse from thousands of available candidates. Taking responsibility for this decision is the first step to owning some of what happened later in the relationship. While we all make mistakes for which we must forgive ourselves and from which we must try to learn, choosing the wrong marriage partner feels more consequential than most.

Here is the fundamental question about our readiness for marriage: Is it possible for us to love another adult as much as we love ourselves? How can we know whether we have the ability to do so? The best indications are how we behave in their presence. Can we truthfully say that we would never do anything intentionally to hurt them? A related and equally important question is, how does this other person make us feel about ourselves? Are we at our best when we are with them?

Then there is our evaluation of the other person's capacity for love. The key qualities we look for here are kindness and a willingness to give of oneself. On the surface the ability to do this may appear to be synonymous with sacrifice, but in the context of a truly loving relationship the line between giving and receiving becomes blurred and the needs and desires of the other person rise to the level of our own.

It is worth noting that what passes for attachment in most marriages more closely resembles a contract in which our willingness to give is related to our perception of how much we are getting from the other person. Such a calculation requires a lot of scorekeeping: I did the grocery shopping last time, now it's your turn. Such a sentiment is an indication that the relationship is in trouble. Likewise, if there is a lot of bargaining around sex, its frequency or methodology, you have a major problem. In this as in all areas of human connection, a cardinal rule applies: *We are entitled to receive only as much as we are prepared to give.*

The conventional wisdom about marriage is that any intimate relationship is hard work and requires a willingness to compromise endlessly. This idea has always seemed to me to be more of a commentary on the marriage of the "expert" offering this platitude than a goal to which couples ought to aspire. At the risk of appearing hopelessly romantic and unrealistic, I maintain that a good marriage is easy provided that both people have been astute in the selection process. If we choose a partner with ample reserves of kindness and a willingness to place us at the center of his or her life, *and* if we have sufficiently cultivated those virtues in ourselves, we can refute the "hard work" school of marriage, put down our picks and shovels, and partake of the endless pleasures of renewable love.

It is easier to be angry than sad.

I t is a standard assumption of pop psychology that the open expression of anger in all areas of our lives, but especially in therapy, is to be encouraged. We wouldn't want people suppressing feelings, after all. Everyone knows how unhelpful—even unhealthy—that can be. So do you have a grievance? Let's hear it. Mad at someone? Let him know about it. If he doesn't like it, that's *his* problem.

This is especially true in couples therapy, where people come in with the idea that somehow expressing unrestrained anger of the sort that is manifest in many bad marriages will "clear the air" and pave the way for reconciliation. Fact: *Anger begets anger*. It is very difficult when one is being attacked to respond reasonably. When I inquire about the way people habitually communicate with each other (and often with their children), what I hear are stories of repetitive conflict in which each person feels a continual need to defend themselves (and we all know the best defense is a good offense). Usually these battles begin with criticism.

I am amazed at how easily and unthinkingly people assume that to live with someone is to be both the target and source of critical comments. "He always leaves his dirty dishes on the counter." Or, "She never gets the oil changed in her car." Or, "The kids just drop their stuff all over the house." And when these things happen, the offended party is not slow to point them out, commonly with intense irritation and frequent use of "always" and "never" for emphasis.

So I ask them, "What would your lives be like if neither of you criticized or gave orders to the other person?" This question is guaranteed to produce skeptical looks all around, as if I had just asked them to stop breathing or never brush their teeth again. What on earth is he talking about? If I didn't point out her mistakes and lack of consideration, I'd be defenseless. The dishes will pile up indefinitely, the oil will never be changed again, the house will sink into chaos.

Here's my argument: If an agreement can be reached to withhold criticism, the emotional tone of the house shifts. The relationship changes from one in which the primary task is keeping score of the other person's transgressions to a cooperative enterprise in which each member of the family has an investment in maintaining enough order that things can be found and guests entertained. What *is* eliminated are the passive-aggressive behaviors that represent the defensive response of people who feel powerless and aggrieved. *Kindness begets kindness.*

This, of course, sounds a lot easier than it turns out to be in practice. What is at work here is the power of habit. Most people grew up in homes in which they were socialized by their parents through the use of "discipline" and criticism. (Alternatively, they were overindulged and never learned the meaning of responsibility.) This sort of upbringing suggests that, left to their own devices, children are agents of disorder and defiance. When speaking about their balky offspring, parents frequently say, "He just doesn't listen!" or, "No matter how many times I tell her, she can't seem to understand the importance of hard work and good grades."

These are the assumptions that promote criticism and

anger as the normal way to relate to those closest to us. By the time people come to see me, they usually have a sense that something is wrong with how they habitually interact. Changing these patterns is another matter. What I see in relationships that are not working is a mutual sadness. This person whom we expected to love forever now annoys us. (If they bore us, that's even worse, but let's stick with anger for the moment.) So behind the power struggles and hostility that are the most evident signs of our discontent lies the profound sadness of failed expectations. This is not what we thought we were signing up for.

Was there ever a time when too little expression of anger constituted a big problem? If so, that time is definitely not now. The country is at war; we worry about road rage; our entertainment presents us with endless images of violence; our favorite spectator sports involve car crashes or men knocking other men senseless. Our national history, indeed the history of the world, is one of unremitting conflict, much of it over what deity to worship. We live in a society with more guns than people.

In fact, it seems to me that just behind the anger that is so evident, and often encouraged, in our lives, are two emotions that are much harder to express: fear and unhappiness. Both of these very common human feelings are seen as weaknesses and are hard to tolerate for long. One way to escape them is to get mad and allocate blame. If we can find a target, we can indulge our outrage and assign responsibility for our misery to someone else. Now we are a victim.

With victimhood comes all sorts of prerogatives, the most important of which is the reassurance that what has happened to us is *not our fault.* We are issued a license to complain (and often a public platform from which to do so). I remember when I found out as an adult that I was adopted. Amid the identity confusion and apprehension that accompanied this shocking revelation was a perverse satisfaction that, after years as a privileged white male, I was now a member of an aggrieved minority group: adult adoptees. I began to publicly complain about the legal barriers to finding out who my birth parents were; I railed against the injustice of being denied my family medical history; I tried (unsuccessfully) to get my state legislature to open adoption records to adults searching for birth parents; I was outraged that newspapers that covered this story persisted in referring to us as "adopted children." I was angry.

Finally, I tired of the struggle and, like many adoptees before and since, searched on my own and found my birthmother. Later I came to feel that the difficult process that this entailed made our reunion that much sweeter for both of us. She knew what I had had to go through to find her, and the search gave me time to both reflect on why I was doing this and deal with the sadness of the long-ago abandonment that required it. But I cannot deny the satisfaction of feeling like an oppressed minority, for a little while at least.

So, the next time you're feeling outraged about something, especially if the target of your anger is someone in your life to whom you long to be closer, ask yourself if this feeling may not be a substitute for some sense of loss or powerlessness. Ask yourself, further, if there might not be something *you* can do that will begin to transform the situation. If you cannot change the people around you, you can at least have the satisfaction of surprising them.

Action is eloquence.

I was standing in the Regimental forward command post when the radio crackled with the news that the Air Cavalry command and control helicopter was on its way to the 93rd Evac Hospital with a casualty on board. I jumped into my jeep and drove the ten minutes to Long Binh, arriving just as the Huey dropped its skids onto the asphalt. Two medics were waiting with a stretcher. I joined them and helped lift the left door gunner onto the gurney. He had been shot in the abdomen and he whispered that he wasn't able to move his legs.

The medics quickly strapped him on and began the run to the receiving area. I started to follow and then looked back at the Huey. Kurland was watching me and there appeared to be a question in his eyes. I knew Heyser would be in surgery in minutes; there was really nothing more I could do for him, so I turned back. As I scrambled in the open door, my boots slipped in his blood. Kurland yanked the helicopter into the air. I plugged back into the intercom and he was on the horn to the Air Cav command post. "I need a door gunner NOW. ETA is three minutes."

As we touched down in a dust storm, a young specialist was running toward us, his flight helmet in his hand. He jumped aboard and blanched at the sight of the blood on the seat in front of the machine gun. He sat down, strapped in, and checked the weapon. We were in the air again, headed back to the scene of contact. Kurland called one of the loaches on station. "Give me a sitrep," he shouted, asking for a situation report.

"OK, boss, we're not taking any more fire. Looks like most of 'em hauled ass. We got two gooks in the open."

"What're they doing?"

"Just sittin' under a tree."

"OK, be there in five."

The hilltop where we had taken fire had been blown apart. The Air Force had apparently paid it a visit; the trees were splintered and the earth cratered. As we came in at seventy-five feet we could see two loaches circling like dragonflies and two cobras orbiting above. Kurland slowed, and sure enough, there were two figures in black sitting with their backs to a tree in the midst of the moonscape. There was no sign of weapons and their heads turned as they watched us pass. "Kill 'em," said Kurland. "Roger that," responded one of the cobra pilots as he banked into his gun run.

"Wait, Frank," I said into the intercom. "They're out of the fight. Why not pick 'em up?" Just then the cobra fired its minigun and the area where the men were sitting exploded in a dust cloud.

"Looks like you're too late, doc."

"Let's land and find out," I replied. I knew he couldn't resist that challenge from his flight surgeon.

He was on the horn again. "Cease fire and cover us. We're going to pick 'em up."

At the base of the hill was a small clearing, barely big enough to drop the Huey in. We knew it would be even trickier to get out of, especially with more weight on board. We left the copilot and crew chief with the idling helicopter while Kurland, I, and the poor door gunner who thirty minutes before had been eating a quiet lunch set off up the hill.

The woods at the bottom were thick and it was not until

we emerged into the open area blasted into the hilltop that we could hear the whip-crack of sniper fire passing overhead. God knows where it was coming from, but we had no way to communicate with the gunships circling above. Kurland and the door gunner had M16s. I had my aid bag and my well-practiced Vietnamese phrase that I planned to use if captured: "*Toi la bac-si*." Would some random VC care that I was a doctor? I doubted it.

As we approached the two bodies under the tree I was amazed to see one of them wave at us. The door gunner was so startled that he fired, missing wildly. "Come on, pal," I said, "do they look ready to fight to you?" Indeed, as we drew closer we could see that one of the men had been hit in the thigh by a round from the cobra. The other, miraculously, was uninjured and stared at us with the stoic resignation of one certain he was about to be executed. The wounded man, more optimistic, signaled with a drinking motion that he wanted water. I gave him my canteen and he swallowed gratefully.

"Let's get the fuck out of here," growled Kurland as he motioned the unhurt VC to get up while I quickly bandaged the wounded man and pulled him to his feet. As I did so he reached back to grab a canvas bag. I looked in it and saw that it was full of medicines, bandages, and notebooks. Apparently, this guy was a medic for his team. We started slowly down the hill, with the nervous door gunner trailing. As he slumped against me, the wounded VC gave no indication of being in pain; indeed, whenever I looked at him he smiled, as if our meeting on this hellish hillside had been pre-arranged.

We got back to the waiting Huey and lifted off. The main rotor clipped some tree branches on the way out and for a moment we thought we were taking fire. Our prisoners looked like people on their first helicopter ride. When we arrived at the regimental command post, I had an argument with the intelligence guys about interrogating the wounded VC before he was evacuated for treatment. As usual with these disputes, I lost, and he was taken away for questioning. Before they dragged him off he smiled at me once more and handed me his aid bag. Inside were notebooks containing exquisite anatomical sketches of things like the brain and the circulatory system. I still have them. I hope he survived the war. If he reads this story, I wish he will let me know so that I can return his drawings.

7

It is better to be spent than saved.

I frequently ask patients, "What are you saving yourself for?" People spend a lot of time conserving energy, usually while they wait for some event outside themselves to trigger their taking action. At times it appears that they are waiting for a reappearance of the Messiah. I always thought that those who feel the rapture is near are fortunate. Not just because they will be saved while the rest of us endure the tribulation, but because they have a good justification to be in a waiting mode, where their main responsibility is praise and worship as they prepare to be transported directly to heaven.

Those of us who lack the comfort of this belief have to come up with other excuses for our inaction. For some people this presents little challenge. Passivity is the enemy of progress in therapy. The conventional medical model in which the doctor gives instructions and medications to patients does not, by itself, work when someone is trying to change his or her life. The process of figuring out what is wrong with our conceptions of how the world works (as opposed to how we would like it to work) and correcting them is, like most educational exercises, time-consuming. It is also frequently uncomfortable as we begin to slowly confront the events and influences that have made us who we are and realize the power of the inertia and habit that stand between us and the people we want to be.

After I published a book of ideas about the human condition a while ago, numbers of people, some of whom lived quite far away, called to set up appointments to consult with me. Having found insight and entertainment from my book, they came with high expectations for the help that I might provide. One of them said, "I've seen a lot of therapists; you're my last chance at mental health." Flattered, I hoped that I would give these patients a new and transformative experience. In fact, what happened is that most of them were disappointed and discontinued therapy after a few sessions. I had not met their expectations as someone who would save them.

I remember John Updike writing that as a young man he was usually disillusioned by meeting writers whose work he admired. They turned out to be drunks, self-important windbags, or otherwise different from the enlightening artists he had expected. And later, when *he* was a writer to be met, he saw the same disappointment in the eyes of those people who now eagerly encountered him. He didn't feel witty or profound enough in person to meet the exaggerated hopes of the admirers of his work.

Those who look outside themselves for direction that will transform their lives are likely to be similarly dissatisfied. The challenge for all of us is to mobilize our own considerable capacity for change, to refine our judgments about what we want and how to get it, and not to imagine that the instructions or conclusions of someone else will rescue us.

In general we can only bring ourselves to the task of change when remaining as we are has become sufficiently painful that we cannot stand it any longer. It begins to dawn on us that life is not a rehearsal. Our time, while uncertain, is finite. People at every age are dying every day, most with a lot of unfinished business.

We all carry around inside ourselves some idea of what

we would like our lives to be. The images of success with which we are bombarded are, in general, both superficial and unattainable. The values of steadfastness and determination do not receive the admiration they deserve. In fact, a consumer society is likely to celebrate the quick solution, the drug that will provide relief, the replacement of the old with the new, the triumph of form over substance. These messages, surrounding us like the air we breathe, produce a lot of confusion about what will make us happy.

Another question I'm fond of asking is, "You seem hesitant about doing things differently; do you consider yourself fragile?" Since the prospect of change is nearly always anxiety-provoking, it's not surprising that people resist it. We are told constantly that an important objective in life is to "chill out"; we hear "don't sweat the small stuff" and "go with the flow." So it's not surprising that people come to regard all anxiety as abnormal and to be avoided. There is, in fact, a huge pharmaceutical industry devoted to fostering the belief that no one should have to tolerate anxiety for longer than it takes to swallow a pill. In some ways this seductive idea has become the basis for the medicalization of human suffering.

A patient who appeared in my office recently was a veteran of several psychiatrists and a consumer of considerable medication. He listed his problems as follows: "anxiety, depression, attention deficit disorder, insomnia, sleep apnea, and narcolepsy." He was, of course, taking antidepressants and anti-anxiety agents. In addition, he was on methamphetamine for ADD and hypnotic medicine to help him sleep. He had had surgery on his soft palate to help with snoring and was hooked up to a positive pressure machine every night to insure that he didn't stop breathing in his sleep. He wasn't much interested in psychotherapy. He had been fully medicalized.

Somewhere in the midst of all this pill-pushing, favored not just by the drug manufacturers but also by the managed-care companies who control reimbursement for mental-health care, we have lost something in our ability to take responsibility for our lives and deal with the inevitable mood changes that are a part of living.

This is not to deny that medication is frequently invaluable to help people deal with mental illness: schizophrenia, bipolar disorder, major depression. Medicines can also help temporarily with problems in living: situational anxiety, grief, post-traumatic stress. But when *the only thing* psychiatrists do for people is medicate them for their intrapsychic discomforts, we have sacrificed something essential in our professional identities. We also convey the message to patients that the passive acceptance of such "treatment" is the preferred method of dealing with emotional problems.

I prefer to challenge people to relinquish passivity, stop waiting for answers outside themselves, mobilize their courage and determination, and try to discover what changes will bring them closer to others and to the people they want to be.

If you have anything to say, say it now,
for the eternal silence is at hand.

I gave the following letter to my youngest daughter at her high school graduation:

Dear Emily,

We come now to what I like to think of as the "silly season," a time of forgettable commencement talks, many of which enjoin young people to "strive for excellence." This seems a worthy goal, but I wish sometimes that one speaker would laud the virtues of competence. In a world where we routinely encounter inadequate performance, I would settle for people simply being good enough at what they do that we are not inconvenienced (or threatened) by their ineptitude.

The tendency to hyperbole is everywhere around us, so that people who can barely carry a tune are introduced as "artists," while those lacking all writing skills are referred to as "authors," and politicians without intelligence or moral standing are our "leaders." This degrading tendency, fostered by a culture of celebrity, not only leads to cynicism and a debasement of taste, it distorts our appreciation of persons of genuine accomplishment. If our heroes shrink, so does our sense of what it is to dare greatly, to truly achieve something. This is one reason I have a fondness for sports. While professional athletes are obscenely overcompensated and frequently flawed human beings, they at least provide us with images of competence and occasionally transcendence.

You know I admire Charles Lindbergh. While it took considerable courage to take off in a single-engine plane across the Atlantic in 1927, the thing I really respect is that he reached the coast of Ireland only three miles off course after flying all night over 1,500 miles of open ocean. While luck certainly played a role, this strikes me as an exceptionally competent piece of navigation. If we all did our jobs that well, the world would run more smoothly. (He also, like me, married well.) His later detour into anti-Semitism was partially redeemed by his twilight concerns for the environment. He aged with grace.

You and I share a belief in skepticism and questioning authority. In situations where survival is the issue: In a lifeboat, when lost in the wilderness, in combat, one learns that *true authority is not arbitrary; it is the natural relationship of knowledge to ignorance.*

So this is a paean to competence. Few of us are able to excel. But it is incumbent on us all (and a definite aid to longevity) to be able adequately to endure, do the work we have chosen, and care for ourselves and those who depend on us.

The value of humor in our lives is another one of those subjects that I feel strongly about but hesitate to raise since you already have such a well-developed ability to laugh and to make others laugh. On many nights your mom and I have turned to each other and smiled when, from behind your closed door, the murmur of a telephone conversation with a friend was punctuated by your contagious laughter. Of the many things I will miss when you leave, this is among the most poignant. At times when my own spirits have flagged, I have often taken strength from your irrepressible optimism and capacity for joy.

Someone once commented "You don't have a sense of humor; it has you." There is truth in that, I think. Often, in the grimmest of situations, I have seen people rise above their fears with laughter. Remember the fake headline we laughed about after 9/11? "America Stronger Than Ever, Say Quadragon Officials."

There is nothing that cannot be lampooned. (Read Jonathan Swift's "A Modest Proposal" sometime.) I, as you know, enjoy making fun of serious people and subjects. Death, for example, gives to life both its urgency and its essential absurdity. Our fondest ideals, strongest passions, and coveted dreams are all eventually dust. That we can still think them important and laugh at their (and our own) transience is, for me, a mark of courage. Another form of humor I love is turning things upside down. My favorite example is Abbie Hoffman's quote from the '60s: "The real question regarding free speech is not whether it is legitimate to yell 'Fire!' in a crowded theater, but whether it is permissible to yell 'Theater!' at a crowded fire."

One description of humans is "the animals that

laugh." This could, of course, be yet another of our conceits. (Perhaps the dogs are laughing at *us* and we just don't get the joke.) But I think it is probable that we are unique among the creatures of the earth in our ability to appreciate our mortality and to choose how seriously to take ourselves.

There are many forms of grace—physical, intellectual, social, spiritual—each of them amazing in its own way. But to cope with inevitable loss, to face life in all its confusion and absurdity and still retain the capacity for joy, laughter, and a belief that our struggles have meaning—this is to prevail.

Love,
Dad

We are defined by what we fear.

Fear is a powerful motivator of behavior that seldom takes us where we want to go. While it is true that people with serious anxiety disorders appear, in many cases, to have a biological predisposition to these conditions, it is also true that anxiety can be learned. Children growing up in families in which one or both parents exhibit a high level of apprehension are often vulnerable themselves to unreasonable fears. The number of adults who are afraid of flying, enclosed spaces, crossing bridges, even driving, is amazingly high. Often, just beneath the surface of an apparent phobia lies an exaggerated sense of the world as a dangerous place.

Once when I was interviewing the parents of an anxious teenager, I inquired if anyone else in the family suffered from irrational worries. The mother replied, "No. We just take prudent precautions, like not taking a shower during a thunderstorm." When I asked if she had ever heard or read of anyone being electrocuted by lightning while in the shower, she replied, "No, but it could happen." This is the attitude about improbable events that supports lotteries. And those who fret about things that will never happen often pass those fears down through the generations.

In a risky world, it is important that we convey to our children an informed assessment of the perils we face. If we can persuade them to fasten their seat belts, wear bike helmets, and not smoke, drink excessively, play with guns, or drive recklessly, we will have armored them against the primary dangers to their physical welfare. If we *really* want to be good parents, we might include a lesson or two on how to recognize people who will break their hearts.

Confronting one's fears is the definition of courage. For a nation that loves to celebrate heroism, America regularly reacts to events like a patient with an anxiety disorder. Immediately after 9/11, a new store opened in New York City. It sold such useful gear as biohazard suits, water purifiers, antibiotics, and parachutes for jumping from a high-rise building. It closed as our panic about terrorist attacks subsided into a chronic apprehension, but that it existed at all is a tribute to the power of our fears.

The media, particularly the 24-hour news shows, bear some responsibility for stoking our worry. What we pay attention to determines how fearful we are. Sometimes it appears that a primary role of the news media is to scare us. Perhaps this is just a way of engaging our attention, but many stories, particularly on the local news, seem designed more to alarm than inform.

A very sensitive index of our fear is sales of handguns. They surged nationwide after 9/11. The absurdity of using a handgun to protect oneself from terrorist attack is beside the point. When we feel threatened, we buy guns. It's what makes us Americans.

Most of us live protected, climate-controlled lives devoted to minimizing risk. When I speak to anxious, depressed patients I often ask them what is the riskiest thing they have ever done. People are surprised. The idea of taking chances has not occurred to most of them. But it is not an idle question. Depression is a "safe" position that many people, miserable as they may feel, are afraid to relinquish. Mobilizing the courage to overcome this inertia is, to an important extent, the work of psychotherapy.

The Native American saying "If we lived forever there would be no such thing as courage" operates here. It is the consciousness of our mortality that marks us as human, that forces us to confront the inevitable loss of ourselves and those we love, to contemplate the great mystery of life with a determination to live as well as we can for as long as we can, unafraid.

When I talk to parents I hear a lot about fears that their children are exposed to dangers they cannot protect them from: drugs in schools, violence in movies, sex on television, predators in the mall or on the Internet. I ask them what effect they think their obsessive worries have on their children. Each year the police in my town offer to X-ray treats handed out on Halloween, looking (vainly so far) for that elusive razor blade in the apple. What messages are we giving our kids about how to live comfortably in the world? It is ironic that in a society often characterized as "child-centered," we should be so heedless of how our futile search for perfect security can transmit the virus of anxiety.

Our frequent demonstrations of patriotism and paeans to those we have designated heroic have the quality of "bravery by proxy." It is as if our public reverence for those who exhibit courage, rather than inspiring each of us to do likewise, serves as a way to feel good without having to do more than bow our heads or wave a flag. This is especially apparent at ceremonies where we observe leaders who have avoided service in the war of their generation solemnly pay homage to those brave (or unlucky) enough to have died on our behalf. We honor these sacrifices while not imagining that any will be required of us.

In some ways it's a miracle that we can tolerate the uncertainties of life without yielding to anxiety or depression. That most of us do so most of the time is both an example of constructive denial and an acknowledgment that the alternative, which is to live in fear, drains life of the pleasures it contains.

Perhaps our most destructive interpersonal anxiety is our fear of intimacy. Some people will do anything to avoid the risks that come with opening oneself fully to another human being. I continually hear lonely people talk about how careful one must be to avoid being hurt. On Internet dating sites the mythical ax murderer plays a prominent role in discouraging contact. Those who have been disappointed in love are preoccupied with protecting themselves from further rejection. Loneliness is often preferred over the vulnerability of closeness.

We have become used to being afraid. Before terrorism threatened us there were killer bees, shark attacks, flu pandemics, sexual predators, and nuclear annihilation. There has never been a shortage of threats or people who wished us ill. We pay money to watch frightening movies. It is even possible to argue that there is a deeply human need to have some symbol of evil in our world that simultaneously frightens and unites us.

We could learn a lot from the citizens of Israel, who live daily with a level of terrorist violence that would (and perhaps will) paralyze us. Based on what's happened so far, try to imagine how our public life would be affected by a few shopping mall explosions or the release of an airborne biotoxin. Somehow we need to mobilize the fortitude to confront the real threats to our well-being and stop scaring ourselves with phantoms.

A patient told me the following story: In 2003 she was at a Baltimore Symphony Orchestra concert. They were playing the Brahms Violin Concerto when suddenly the lights went out. In the utter blackness of the concert hall her immediate thought was that Baltimore was under terrorist attack, a fear no doubt shared by many in that audience. She is uncertain how long they were in darkness before the dim emergency lights came on—probably only a few seconds, though it seemed longer. What amazed her was that *the orchestra kept playing.* Sitting in the dark, unable to see the conductor or their scores, the musicians played on, flawlessly. No one in the crowd made a sound, though she remembers the ovation at the end of the piece as especially heartfelt.

We are not often called upon to demonstrate courage by risking our lives. But in numberless acts of quiet determination in the face of the anxiety that now infects this society, we perform a service to our country and to each other. Collectively, our attitudes and behavior create the atmosphere we live in and, more than any military action, will ultimately determine the outcome of the struggle with terror in which we are now engaged. In the process we might at last find something in ourselves of which we can be truly proud.

The best stepparents do the least parenting.

What with all the divorce and remarriage these days, there are a lot of people raising other people's children. It doesn't always go smoothly. When children of divorce are interviewed, most of them say that their deepest desire is to have their parents back together, even if they know that the marriage was an unhappy one. While it is customary for people to rationalize that raising children in a home with a lot of parental conflict is a poor idea, kids almost universally want their parents together and entertain reunion fantasies for a long time after it is apparent that this is not going to happen.

The most visible reminder that the divorce is final is a parent's remarriage. Actually, this event is often difficult for the adults involved as well. I remember when I was informed by my former wife two years after our divorce that she was getting married again. We had done what we could to remain on friendly terms on behalf of the children, so the best response to her impending marriage that I could come up with was, "You know, we met each other and fell in love, then we married, then we had children, then we fell out of love and got divorced, then I remarried, now you're getting remarried. I feel like we're drifting apart."

If the divorce has been a bitter one and the children have been used as pawns, the risk is even greater that they will have difficulty accepting any new parental figures. "You're not my father!" or "You're not my mother!" are responses many stepparents are familiar with in response to their attempts to impose discipline. Contained in these protests is all the pain of children who have suffered the disillusionment of their parents' divorce, resentment at the back and forth of visitation schedules, and the divided loyalties imposed on them by the continuing acrimony between the adults they love most. It's much easier and emotionally safer to be angry at a stepparent than at either of one's real parents.

Meanwhile, stepparents are typically struggling with their own difficulties learning to love someone else's children and frustration at the ambiguous roles they have been asked to play. Commonly, they have a different philosophy of parenting than their spouses and have to reconcile this while coping with the oppositional, frequently hostile reactions of children whose lives have been turned upside down. In the case of "blended families," in which each partner has brought children into a second marriage, things are even more complicated, with allegations of favoritism toward one's own children becoming a big issue.

So what strategy works best for someone put in the position of relating to someone else's kids? In my experience, the best stepparenting strategy is to *leave the discipline to the child's parent.* This may require some tongue-biting, particularly if the stepparent feels provoked or believes that the real parent is too lax in setting rules. "What am I supposed to do if the kid is acting out and my husband isn't there?" Answer: nothing; it's not your problem. Any stepparent intervention will be resented by the child, and the resultant conflict is harmful to the establishment of a respectful and affectionate relationship between stepparent and child.

Why do you suppose that the standard fairy-tale villainess is the "wicked stepmother"? Because this is not a new story, and stepparents have always been accorded second-class status by children. Who is the typical perpetrator of child sexual abuse? It's the stepfather. Again, the cultural assumption is that one cannot love another person's child as one's own.

It should go without saying that stepparents should *never* be drawn into criticism of either of the child's actual parents. The bitterness that can be produced by such commentary is obvious. Kids, in general, are very protective of their parents and react with defensiveness if they think that a stepparent is trying to replace a real parent. The whole issue of what a child should call the stepparent can be thorny. Using one's first name is generally a good choice. Any attempt to get the child to use "Dad" or "Mom" when referring to a stepparent can provoke explosive resistance in children.

The stepparent strategy that works in most cases is to try to establish a friendly, nondisciplinary relationship in which one is emotionally available but declines to get caught up in typical parent/child conflict. This can profitably be left to the child's real parent. Most stepparents who adopt this approach experience relief at not feeling responsible for correcting, teaching, disciplining, or otherwise parenting a resentful child. When I talk to adults who, as children, lived with stepparents, the greatest compliment they are able to give is: "She was always there for me." In other words, freed of the boundary-setting tasks of parenthood, the good step-parent is able to give the child something unique: a friendly, nonjudgmental adult perspective on the world.

Most guides to stepparenting follow the standard advice for all human relationships: *It's hard, stressful work, so buckle down to it and pray for strength.* It's amazing to me that so few advice-givers ever say, "Life in general and good relationships with other human beings in particular don't have to be difficult. In fact, if they are, maybe you need to reevaluate your approach." I often think that the entire self-help industry depends on a "Life is hard, then you die" worldview. If that's the case, then of course you need lots of guidance and advice. This may sell books, but I think it keeps people's expectations low and their stress levels high. Stepparenting is a subset of this philosophy. If you anticipate that it will require constant work, ironclad discipline, and frequent conflict-resolution exercises, then you have bought into a self-fulfilling prediction. If, on the other hand, you can relax, find a little humor, and exercise your friendship-forming abilities, you might just find that being with another person's children is not quite the onerous experience that everyone makes it out to be.

I wish to acknowledge here that virtually everything I know about step-parenting (and other forms of love) was taught to me by my wife, Clare.

*One of life's most difficult tasks is to see
ourselves as others see us.*

Most people hate mirrors. I think that's because when we look in one we experience a profound dissatisfaction. Who is that person? When did I get so old? Where did those wrinkles come from? Who besides a mother could love that face? Few of us approximate the conventional ideal of physical beauty, and we dislike being reminded of this.

A lot of people despise their imperfections and are willing to spend a lot of money to conceal or repair them. It is also apparent that we tend to judge others by their most superficial characteristics. On Internet dating sites people talk about their interests and accomplishments, but it is their age and picture that primarily determine the response their profiles evoke. (There is some gender difference here, with surveys suggesting that women are more interested in the kind of job men have than what they look like.)

Once we begin to know people, other personality characteristics take on more importance. Still, our view of ourselves seldom comports accurately with the way we are seen by others. Most people, for example, see themselves as honest, reliable, and empathetic. In my experience, these laudable characteristics are not uniformly distributed in the population. In fact, when people respond to group crises, it usually turns out to be a minority who behave well.

There was, for example, an accident that occurred in Baltimore's inner harbor a couple of years ago. A gust of wind capsized a water taxi with about twenty people on board. This occurred in early spring so the water was cold. When rescue boats appeared on the scene, most of the passengers were on top of the overturned pontoon boat shouting that there were people trapped underneath. No one, apparently, asked the logical question, "Then why are you standing on top?" When the rescuers finally lifted one pontoon, three bodies floated out, one of them that of a child.

Who among us can say how we would behave in such a

situation? We would like to think that we would behave bravely, especially if the lives of children are at stake. Yet there are enough examples of panic in the face of danger to make us wonder if we have it in us to act unselfishly.

Even in more mundane situations not involving great risk, it is sometimes hard to find people who are willing to behave in ways contrary to their self-interest. I was asked some years ago to testify in a child-custody case in which I had evaluated both parents. In the course of therapy it came out that the mother had engaged in a homosexual relationship outside the marriage. Her husband was trying to use this allegation against her in an effort to gain custody. His attorney was pressing me to confirm that this was true.

I felt that my professional obligation was to not say anything that would injure either my patients or their children; I also did not think her affair had affected her parenting. So I declined to answer the question on the grounds of doctor/patient confidentiality. The judge sternly reminded me that child custody was an exception to this privilege under Maryland law and that he could "compel" me to answer. I looked around for the thumbscrews but realized that he was simply threatening to cite me for contempt and send me to jail.

What was interesting to me was that this jurist had no understanding of the ethical quandary in which I found myself. It was obvious that he was so accustomed to seeing people behave in their own self-interest that he could not conceive of someone acting otherwise. To him I was simply an annoying obstacle to the smooth functioning of his court, and he could not imagine that I would risk jail by defying him. As it happened, my client, seeing the threat, waived privilege and allowed me to testify, but I still reflect on the meaning of that judge's assumption that anyone can be bullied.

Whatever the failure of our good intentions, the road to hell is paved with hypocrisy. How often does it occur to us that there is a disconnect between how we see ourselves and how we are seen by others? Much of the self-righteousness and antagonism we feel toward those who differ with us is attributable to a kind of blindness that affects our perception of our own faults.

The process of therapy, of course, attracts people whose lives are in trouble. Apart from the routine confrontations with anxiety and depression, every therapist is faced daily with people whose desire to live comfortably in the world is impeded by a need to disguise their real impulses and behaviors. The marital wreckage that flows from infidelity, the unwillingness to give another person the affection we would like to receive from them, the general disparity between what we say and what we do, all contribute predictably to the demise of our closest relationships.

The stories that people tell me of their upbringing are not typically full of admiration for their parents. If there is a single arena in which hypocrisy does the most damage, it is parenthood. Here the stakes are highest. The disparity between word and action is on its most egregious display in families, where it is most difficult to disguise what it is that we truly believe in. The stories of parental alcoholism; verbal, physical, and sexual abuse; neglect; and selfishness are heartbreaking in their frequency in the life stories of people who are struggling to do better with their own children than their parents did with them.

Is it too much to ask of ourselves to move through life inflicting as little damage on others as possible? It does no good to argue that we have done the best that we could if those who were there have a dissenting view. It also matters little whether we damage others unintentionally or with malice aforethought. If one is run over by a truck, the intentions of the driver are, to the victim, irrelevant. Nor can we, in general, plead ignorance of the effects of our behavior on those placed in our care. Parenthood is a sacred trust, and we must all take to our graves the judgment of the people closest to us.

12

*Moral certainty is the reward
of the true believer.*

*Now faith is the assurance of things hoped for, the conviction of
things not seen.*

—Hebrews 11:1

G rowing up Catholic in the 1940s and '50s was an exercise in the management of fear. I felt controlled by the
Church with a promise of salvation based on a series of prohibitions and threatened punishments that ensured that I
remained tractable, anxious, and guilt-ridden.

The idea that I found most intimidating was the oft-repeated equivalency of "thought, word, and deed." No allowance was made for the uncontrollable nature of fantasies and feelings. Instead, the failure to restrain them was seen as not simply a precursor to sin, but sin itself. The Church's marketing genius was evident in that the only avenue of escape for our immortal souls was through the sacrament of confession.

Each week I sat outside the confessional, racking my brain for sins that would be convincing but not require a penance longer than a couple of rosaries. I imagined that if I exposed the deplorable depths of my youthful imagination, nothing short of a public flogging would suffice to expiate such sin. I regularly confessed to having inadvertently eaten meat on Friday, which had the advantage of being both a mortal sin and somehow erasable with a few Our Fathers and Hail Marys.

Once a year in the Church of St. Paul the Apostle, the congregation was required to stand and recite the pledge of the Legion of Decency, the arm of the Church that decreed which books and movies were off-limits to the faithful. It was on a Sunday at age sixteen that I made what was to be a final break with the Catholic faith of my mother by refusing to rise and swear that I would abide by the Legion's proscriptions.

As it happened, I was, in my sex-crazed adolescent state, determined to see the recently released film *The Outlaw* ("SENSATION Too Startling To Describe!") that featured a scene of Jane Russell climbing into bed, fully clothed, with Billy the Kid (Jack Beutel). In truth, it was the effect produced by the Howard Hughes–designed suspension-bridge bra worn by Miss Russell that seemed most interesting to me at the time.

The desire to see a movie may seem a trivial reason to break with the faith in which one has been raised, but there it is. I think I was just tired of feeling guilty about thoughts and impulses that I knew were widely shared. (I, of course, never realized then how much they were shared—and sometimes acted upon—by the priests who so controlled our spiritual lives.)

When I went to West Point, church on Sunday was a required event, so I chose to march to the Protestant chapel, where the music was better, no one recited Latin, and "Onward, Christian Soldiers" had literal relevance. A few years later I found myself in Vietnam.

I suppose I shouldn't have been surprised that the Chaplains Corps, like the Medical Corps, was a wholly owned subsidiary of the military and concerned itself with providing a kind of theological justification for the task at hand instead of simply ministering to the souls of the soldiers. It was customary to close each evening's briefing with a prayer. One night, our commanding officer, Col. George S. Patton III, turned to the chaplain and asked him, "What shall we pray for tonight, Chaplain? How about a big body count?" The chaplain obliged as follows: "Help us, O Lord, to fulfill the standing order of the regiment. Let us find the bastards, then pile on."

Of all the stories with which to regulate our lives, why not choose the one that inflicts the least damage on other people? The problem with most deeply held faith is that it requires of its adherents that they view their particular solution to the puzzle of life as the only valid one. Apart from the arrogance of such an assumption, among fundamentalists there is frequently a belief that one therefore has the right to impose one's answers on others.

In its most joyful form, this urge to proselytize becomes an effort to "share the good news" of salvation. The advantage of this approach from the point of view of society at large is that those not interested can change the channel; no one is required to listen. Unfortunately, people who are filled with the Holy Spirit are often not satisfied simply to persuade. Sooner or later the need to coerce others into listening becomes manifest. Thus, they have a need to inflict public, sectarian prayer on students; or begin athletic contests and graduations by invoking Jesus; or insist on having "under God" included in the great secular religion that is patriotism.

Even if we were all only bullied into listening to the public prayers of the faithful (why, one wonders, does an omnipotent God require such frequent praise?), things would not be intolerable. But, of course, words are not enough. If one is privy to the revealed truth, those who will not listen must be *forced* to conform to the word of God. It is not enough that the benighted will lose their souls and their chance at eternal life; they must first lose the right to live in *this* world according to their own lights.

The theme that runs through any coercive fundamentalist belief, whether it is in the God of Islam or the God of the Old Testament, is that ultimately our social and governmental structures must correspond to the precepts of the Koran or the Bible (as interpreted by the true believers). The Taliban in Afghanistan and the mullahs in Iran have given us a glimpse of what such a society, one in which the church *is* the state, looks like. It is not a pretty picture and resembles, interestingly, the social structure of atheistic Communism as interpreted by the Soviet leadership in the twentieth century.

The essence of democracy (and, coincidentally, of mental health) is freedom of choice, the choice to live one's life as one pleases as long as it does not impinge on the rights of others. The core of fundamentalist belief, however, is limitation of choice ("Thou shalt not . . ."). Not for the faithful are the gray areas of moral relativism that they deplore in "secular humanism." They insist on the moral absolutes expressed in their particular interpretation of the Bible.

Deeply religious people are, by definition, certain that they are right about the fundamental questions of human existence. It is in the nature of those imbued with faith to have complete confidence in the (unprovable) reality of a particular deity and total certainty about their interpretation of some set of religious writings that purport to reveal God's will.

For some reason, perhaps the human love of a good story, it also appears necessary to create a metaphysical adversary for our chosen divinity, an embodiment of evil that, out of pure, unexplained corruption, competes for our allegiance and immortal souls. It is this cosmic conflict that gives rise to the two-alternatives view of human events that has such destructive implications for relationships between people and nations in a diverse, ambiguous world.

This is, as much as anything, the "lesson of 9/11": The defining belief of the suicide bombers was that they were engaged in a profoundly religious act, striking at the secular heart of the infidels. Their degree of certitude cannot be doubted, and their last words almost certainly were *"Allah Akbar,"* God is great.

The spirit of democracy rests on the conviction that no one has a corner on the truth. We are all fallible human beings, struggling to create a world in which we respect the right of others to frame their own beliefs about life's large questions in the way that seems best to them. If there is an existence beyond this one, it cannot be in a place that admits only a tiny fraction of humanity based on an accident of birth or faith.

In the long history of mankind many stories have been created to explain the origin and purpose of life, to comfort us in the face of the misfortune and unfairness that surround us, and to give us hope in the face of the death that is our common fate. One longs for a story that would promote the idea that our conceptions of God and his role in our lives are varied and culturally determined. Whatever one's image of heaven, hell on earth is created by attempts to coercively promote one set of beliefs over another. I long for the emergence of a faith whose core doctrine endorses humility and tolerance. The principal idea behind such a Church would be that God values good works over piety. And the essential commandment would be: "Thou shalt keep thy religion to thyself."

Relinquish dignity last.

Fact: In the United States there are now thirty-five million people over the age of sixty-five, 13 percent of the population. Their numbers are increasing and, with the reluctant help of the baby-boom generation, there will be seventy million elderly by 2030.

For obvious reasons, I've been paying more attention to the aging process lately. As a psychiatrist, I see a selected sample of the elderly, but I also have the experience of friends and contemporaries to draw upon. It's not, in general, an attractive prospect.

One of the risks we run throughout life is that of becoming a cultural cliché. We can do this at any age: the rebellious teen, the naïve newlywed, the acquisitive yuppie, the overburdened parent, the cautious midlifer, the indolent retiree. But it is in the final stage of life that we are most at risk of surrendering to the depredations of time and loss and becoming the irrelevant aged whom we pitied in our youth.

The passing of the years strips us of many of the pretenses with which we disguise our true selves. Of all that we fear, it is infirmity and death that terrify us the most. The billions of dollars spent on cosmetics, reconstructive surgery, and an absurd collection of "food supplements" bear testimony to our futile attempts to expunge the visible evidence of our mortality. What we need, of course, is the courage to face (so to speak) what we have become: old.

Marginalized by society, tolerated by adult children who can bear our company only in small doses, the elderly tend to live with others who also have more leisure than imagination. When jobs and family responsibilities are at an end, we run the risk of becoming extraneous, both to society and to ourselves.

This, I think, is why the old have such a deserved reputation as complainers. If we become preoccupied with our physical selves when we are young, we are thought of as hypochondriacs. When we think (and speak) primarily of our aches when we are old, we are just bad company. I frequently encounter adult children who dread conversations with their parents simply because they know they will be subjected to a litany of infirmities that they have already heard many times before. Nothing could be less interesting, even in someone we love, than a repetitious recitation of ailments that are beyond the reach of both medical science and the trapped listener. If boring others is not enough, what happens when we start to bore ourselves?

I see one middle-aged woman who has grown so tired of listening to complaints and unsolicited advice from her mother that when they have a phone conversation, she holds the receiver at arm's length so that she can hear the sound of her mother's voice but can't quite make out the words. When her mother stops talking, the woman says, "Yes, Mom," into the receiver and holds it out again as her mother goes on. And on. And on. I have actually recommended this technique to some desperate adult children whose conversations with their parents are devoid of what is usually meant by the word *communication.*

As we age, our physical world shrinks, and often so does our range of enthusiasms. It is amazing to me, for example, how few older people I encounter who are computer literate. In one survey of people over sixty-five, only 31 percent had *ever* been online, even to send and receive e-mail. (The corresponding figure for the next generation of elderly, now fifty to sixty-five, was 70 percent.) To have television as one's primary window on the world is almost unbearably sad.

Among the criticisms of my previous book was that it did not contain sufficient instructions to be worthy of its place in the self-help section of bookstores. Here are a few suggestions for those whose wishes for longevity have been granted:

1. Stop complaining. A couple of generations earlier, you would have been dead for ten years.
2. If you don't have an activity in your life that causes you to lose track of time, you need to find something.
3. If you go to the doctor more than ten times per year and don't have a terminal illness, get a new hobby.
4. It's true that they haven't written any good music for thirty years. Neither your children nor your grandchildren want to hear about it.
5. If anyone wants to know what life was like when you were their age, they'll ask.
6. Don't worry about avoiding temptation. As you grow older, it will avoid you.
7. Never mind dying with dignity; try living with dignity.

Though much is taken, much abides.

Chances of getting a crew slot in the biennial Transpac race from L.A. to Honolulu at age 70 are slim. So, in 2003, Lloyd Sellinger did what any self-respecting septuagenarian wanting a ride to Hawaii would do: He lied about his age. "I told the skipper, a man in his 40s, that I was 69; it sounded better." When he was turned down anyway, Lloyd came up with the perfect revenge. He would prepare his own 40-foot sailboat for the 2005 Transpac and require that every member of the crew be over 65.

When his intentions were published in a California sailing magazine, he immediately started getting applicants. Andy Szaz, 67, called first. A member of the 1956 Hungarian Olympic team in the Finn class, Andy had been a yacht broker for 25 years and campaigned his Peterson 30 out of Newport Beach. That the name of the boat is *Babe* tells you all you need to know about Andy.

Mike Gass, 66, is an optometrist living with his wife on his 42-foot ketch, *Suzannah*, on the same dock in Seal Beach where Lloyd keeps his boat, though they had never before met. He signed on next as navigator.

Herb Huber, 67, a general contractor/engineer from San Francisco, veteran of numerous sailing campaigns who now sails his Ericson 35 on San Francisco Bay, and Jim Doherty, 67, a communications relay installer, grandfather of thirteen and owner of an Islander 36 in Los Angeles, were the next two crew members accepted after sailing auditions.

That's when I heard about the adventure in far-off Maryland and applied. Lloyd by that time had several other likely prospects so he told me he'd keep my résumé on file. Lucky for me, the other candidates either broke things when they sailed on the boat, had visible tremors, or insisted on scurrying to the foredeck on their hands and knees. Lloyd e-mailed me and I flew to L.A. in January 2005 for a trial sail. I emphasized my 35-year racing experience in small boats but played down the fact that I had sailed nothing larger than thirty feet and had never been out of sight of land in a sailboat. The fact that I was an M.D. weighed in my favor, though the detail that my specialty is psychiatry raised some (mostly unspoken) concerns.

The practice sail went well. I knew port from starboard, didn't fall overboard, and appeared likely to survive two weeks at sea; I was selected as the last of what came to be known as "The Dirty Half-Dozen." I agreed to fly to California monthly to practice or race before the Transpac in July. I also promised to brush up on physical and emergency medicine and to stop referring to all potential ailments and injuries as "psychosomatic." Most important, we all seemed to get along. There were no abrasive personalities or people who thought they knew everything. In retrospect, Lloyd's intuitive crew-selection process and his easygoing leadership style proved sound; there was not a harsh word exchanged among us in our six-month campaign. Though no one had known anyone else on board at the beginning, we were all friends at the end.

Once our effort got a little publicity we, of course, had to deal with the Viagra jokes. Was the drug company going to sponsor us? (No, but we had asked.) Finally, we came up with a satisfactory response: we were taking some Viagra pills with us on the trip, but only to keep us from rolling out of our bunks.

A long ocean voyage, like any quest, is both an expression of hope and a journey within, undertaken for reasons that turn out to have little to do with the outcome. In our early practice sails and in our races to Mexico and around Santa Barbara Island, we learned a couple of things. First, we were slow. Our 1969 Cal 40, *Bubala* (Yiddish for "Sweetheart"), and dated sail inventory made it unlikely that we could keep up with lighter boats, more experienced crews, and bigger budgets. Second, it didn't make any difference. We were there to sail to Hawaii as fast as we could. None of us had Transpac experience. This was going to be the trip of a lifetime, and for us perfect speed meant being there.

The 2,500-mile race began off Point Fermin, west of Los Angeles. The winds were light and got lighter as the day wore on. Under normal conditions we would have expected to pass Catalina Island at five in the afternoon. Instead we ghosted at 2 knots past the blinking light at the west end about two the next morning. Just beyond Santa Barbara Island we fell into a glassy calm that lasted nearly eight hours. On the evening of day 2 we were pushed by the current more than a mile back toward the mainland. Finally, a light breeze filled in and we made what turned out to be a terrible decision to sail north of San Nicolas Island, the last outpost of the North American continent before the open Pacific. As we approached the island at night we elected to sail farther north past some rock outcroppings. The wind shifted and suddenly we were close-hauled on a course to the northwest that pointed us approximately toward the Aleutian Islands. By the time we were able to tack back and round the rocks, we had lost hours on boats that had gone south into stronger winds.

At about this time we discovered that some new batteries that had been installed on the boat were not accepting a charge properly. This failure required us to shut down all lights and restrict our radio communications to the morning position report and evening "bed check." It also disrupted plans to call our families via shortwave radio and meant that we could not receive weather faxes on our computer.

Once we adjusted to the watch system, three hours on/three hours off, we settled into the experience. For me the immensity of the ocean was a lesson in personal insignificance. It was impossible to contemplate that environment without an acute consciousness of our vulnerability. We had food to eat, water to drink, and each other to talk to, but we saw no other signs of human activity—no boats, not even an airplane—for fourteen days. Others, especially single-handed sailors, experience much more profound isolation, but for me this was enough of a reminder of our remoteness, powerlessness, and dependence upon the unpredictable movement of air.

A ship, Samuel Johnson opined, is like a prison, with the added prospect of being drowned. In fact, a small boat on the high seas is a microcosm of the human experience: loneliness, cooperation, and an abiding belief that through skill, determination, and luck we can overcome forces whose power dwarfs our own. We are a speck of consciousness in a universe utterly indifferent to our fate. Yet we may win through and find land and others of our kind.

Once we got into the northeast trade winds we reassured ourselves that this was one of the most reliable weather systems on earth; still, we prayed they would hold. At some moments we were at the edge of our abilities as the wind velocity crept close to 30 knots, and we boiled along at maximum hull speed, higher when we surfed the following seas. Holding a course with the spinnaker up at night under those conditions required a sort of dance at the helm, balancing precariously between a broach in one direction and a disastrous jibe in the other.

A race across the Pacific in the twilight of life is a compelling metaphor for how best to confront the western horizon—flat out, spinnaker drawing, dolphins leaping alongside, in the company of kindred spirits. What could be better than this?

We celebrated the halfway mark with champagne and reflected on the fact that we were then at a point farther from land than anywhere on the planet. We stopped listening to position reports from the other boats because they did nothing for our morale; nor could they help in our planning. The trade winds were up and down but never deserted us wholly, and on the evening of our fifteenth day we saw the glow of lights on Maui. We had only to change course once more at Molokai and head for the finish, thirty-two miles away. But first, it turned out, we had to defy death one last time.

The choice had been made to fly a relatively small spinnaker that had come with the boat in the '60s. As we approached Molokai at night in 25-knot winds, the sail became progressively harder to manage and ultimately wrapped itself on the forestay. All hands turned to in an attempt to get it down. Three were on the foredeck and three in the cockpit when the helmsman became distracted, and with a sound I will never forget, the wind caught the mainsail at its rear edge and threw it in an instant from one side of the boat to the other. As the boom whistled over my head, my first thought was that someone was dead, overboard, or else the mast was gone. As it happened, none of these disasters occurred, and so we subdued the spinnaker and, under a waning moon, sailed on into the dawn.

As we drew abreast of Oahu the sun rose behind us and bathed Diamond Head in the pristine glow of a new day. With the old Eagles barnburner, "Already Gone," playing on the iPod, the years slipped away, and for a moment it was possible to feel the strength of our younger selves. We finished more than two days behind the first boat in our class; we suffered from a failure of speed but not of the heart or of the spirit. We were, finally, six old men on an old boat racing toward the embrace of those who loved us and in whose eyes we were already heroes.

> . . . Come, my friends,
> 'Tis not too late to seek a newer world.
> Push off, and sitting well in order smite
> The sounding furrows; for my purpose holds
> To sail beyond the sunset, and the baths
> Of all the western stars, until I die.
> It may be that the gulfs will wash us down:
> It may be we shall touch the Happy Isles,
> And see the great Achilles, whom we knew.
> Tho' much is taken, much abides; and tho'
> We are not now that strength which in old days
> Moved earth and heaven; that which we are, we are,
> One equal temper of heroic hearts,
> Made weak by time and fate, but strong in will
> To strive, to seek, to find, and not to yield.

—Alfred, Lord Tennyson, *Ulysses*

The important questions
are unanswerable.

Pe_ople bring many questions to psychotherapy. The process itself involves the Socratic method of Q&A. It is the therapist's job to formulate additional questions, not in the expectation of receiving definitive answers, but in the hope that the person seeking help, in trying to respond, will think about his or her life in ways that will enable him to change it for the better.

Unfortunately, in the public mind, therapists are expected to provide advice. It's easy to see where this misconception comes from. Those who appear on television and write self-help books generally put themselves forward as possessed of special wisdom and experience that qualifies them to tell others how to live their lives, raise their children, and manage their relationships. So it's not unusual for patients in the early stages of therapy to tell their story and ask, "What should I do?" Sometimes the request is even more specific: "Do you think I should divorce this guy?" In general, patients don't want this question thrown back at them, as in, "What do *you* think you should do?" They assume that I know but for some obscure reason want them to come to the conclusion for themselves. The fact is, of course, I *don't* know.

To assume that people have within themselves the capacity to decide what is best for them is a vote of confidence. This is my problem with television therapists. Though their advice usually sounds sensible, it presupposes both that they know the person in front of them, whom they have usually just met, well enough to decide what is in their best interests, *and* that this person could not come up with a better solution on their own. The difficulty, of course, is that real therapy takes time and doesn't make for good television, while advice can be given immediately. If what the therapist says makes sense to the audience, they applaud; the person seeking help nods in agreement and the problem is wrapped up in minutes. There is seldom much follow-up to see what actually happened.

There is a hierarchy to the questions we ask ourselves. The trivial involve day-to-day decisions: What errands shall I run? What color should I paint my bedroom? Paper or plastic? The questions at the next level involve more consequential issues: Where shall I live? Whom shall I marry? What work suits me? Finally, the large questions hang in the background: How can I derive meaning from my life? What happens to us when we die? Why do bad things happen to good people?

It is the second-level questions that constitute most of the grist for the therapeutic mill, though the focus is generally on symptoms: Why am I sad most of the time? Why do certain situations make me anxious? Why am I angry with the person I'm married to? Why are my children misbehaving? It is in the course of trying to find answers to these questions that we often find ourselves discussing the meaning of life, even though these greater questions are traditionally the province of religion and do not directly address the more practical concerns that people think about when they come for relief of emotional discomfort.

And yet our lives and our happiness turn out to be inextricably entwined with the large questions of meaning. The fact that they can't be answered in any definitive way applicable to all is what makes the search for answers so important. The awareness of our mortality, for example, is what gives time its import and urgency. We know that "living happily ever after" is only for people in fairy tales. The rest of us are on a more restricted schedule and our challenge is to use our limited time as well as we can.

We want for ourselves whatever we imagine will make us happy. Accumulation of money turns out to be a frequent objective, though it is not clear that people who have lots of it are measurably happier than those with less. We also carry around fantasies of endless excitement and are displeased when that too proves elusive. When people wonder why some among us choose to use drugs that ultimately destroy their lives, I always think the answer is obvious: these substances make people feel good in a way that is hard to replicate elsewhere. (I used to carry Post-it notes with me and, when I came across a car in a parking lot with the bumper sticker HUGS ARE BETTER THAN DRUGS, I left a note on the windshield asking, "But have you tried both?")

The most persistent fantasy is the search for perfect love. Hollywood has done its part in fueling this chimera, and people engage in what turns out in most cases to be a disappointing quest for the person who will save them with the unqualified approval and support that is our deepest wish. Seldom does this search take the form of asking the really important question: What can I make of myself that would make me worthy to give and receive such love? We want to bask in the warmth of devotion that overlooks, even indulges, our failings. Apart from our mothers, this pleasure can be a little hard to find—or to maintain over time.

What I am suggesting is that to focus our lives around the small or medium-sized questions and ignore the large ones is not a likely path to getting what we want. It is like looking at (or painting) a picture and concentrating exclusively on the foreground. It is spirituality that serves as the background and frame for our existence. We can hew to a religious dogma (any one will do) and hang around with those who believe similarly, or we can try to find elsewhere tentative answers that will enable us to make sense of our lives and live them in accordance with our deepest values. Whether or not we will be rewarded in heaven, we will at least have something to guide us through the confusing maze we must daily navigate. It is only when we are too obtuse, frightened, or distracted to ask the important questions that we are truly lost.

Attachment is the source of all suffering.

It is impossible to comprehend the experience of grief with mere words. And yet what else do we have to help each other understand it? There are no "tricks" or pat solutions or foolproof techniques that enable one to comfort a grieving person. This is because, like our faces and our personalities, our individual responses to terrible loss are various. While there are things you should *not* say, there are no words that are guaranteed to soothe. It is our presence with the grieving person that provides the best hope of comfort, our willingness to be with them, to listen to their pain, to share their sense of helplessness.

It is not good to go through grief alone. And often those close to us who seem the logical candidates to be with us are so wounded and caught up in their own experience of loss that they can think only of themselves. This is why children who have lost a sibling often feel abandoned by their grieving parents. And it is at least part of the reason why parents who have lost a child divorce with such frequency.

Death is our great enemy because it mocks our illusions of control as it routinely renders us powerless. Even when it is expected—in hospice, in nursing homes—it still frightens us. How much worse when it comes unexpectedly in birthing rooms and delivery suites, places designed for joy. Here is where our courage is really tested.

Our best hopes for the future repose in our children-to-be. They are the ones who will love us as only a child can, who will carry our genes into the next generation, who will blossom into happy adults, who will care for us when we are old. Even before we know them, they are a part of us. They have already, while still unborn, changed our view of ourselves and of our place in the world. Whether or not we have other children, these new babies occupy a huge space in our lives. Already we take it as our most pleasurable obligation to protect them from harm. We imagine them slowly, with our help, becoming their own people.

While the dreams we have for our own lives have undergone the shrinkage and alteration imposed on us by our experience of the world, the dreams that we dream for our unborn children are limitless and pure. Untested by reality, they exist in the realm of endless possibility, where youth and beauty reign, where hearts are not broken, where age brings only wisdom, and where time is not our enemy.

These children will be brilliant in ways that we are not. They will do well in school. They will live under our protection until they are ready to bear their own children, our grandchildren, who will also be in their own ways flawless. These children have the perfection of an untested promise and we love them already. The day we finally get to meet them is meant to contain all the joy and fulfillment of which human beings are capable.

The nursery is ready, the colorful mobile hangs over the newly purchased crib. The changing table and diapers are there. The soothing color of the walls has been chosen and the rocking chair where the baby will be nursed stands ready. There is a music box at hand ready to play a familiar lullaby. The car seat in which the baby will ride home from the hospital is installed. There is family in the waiting room or sitting by the phone, ready to celebrate its newest member.

And then . . . we are baptized in the icy water of sudden death and unimaginable pain. What is worse is the growing awareness that we will never again be the same people, that this is a loss that is irredeemable, that it will never go away, that the best we can hope for is a sort of numbed standoff with our fate. Whatever else we are or will become, we will henceforth be a parent bereaved. A great wave of loneliness and despair sweeps over us and we struggle to draw breath. It would be merciful, we think, if our hearts stopped now.

No one teaches us how to grieve or how to be with those who are grieving. Some people seem more able to comfort those who mourn, but then some people are better than others at all sorts of human interactions. Perhaps we can all get better at it by understanding the process and what we bring to it from our own life experience.

Grief and mourning are surrounded by myth. First of all, people use the terms synonymously, although they are actually different experiences. Grief is the thoughts and feelings experienced within oneself upon the death of someone loved. It is the internal experience of bereavement. Mourning is the taking of the internal experience of grief and expressing it outside of ourselves. This is a very culture-bound process. Contemporary American culture is focused on one imperative: Get over it. The section on bereavement in the *Diagnostic and Statistical Manual of Mental Disorders* of the

American Psychiatric Association contains the following sentence: "The diagnosis of Major Depressive Disorder is generally not given unless the symptoms are still present two months after the loss." In other words, you have two months to grieve, and after that, if you're not back to your old self, you have a mental illness.

Another common myth is that there is an orderly progression through the experience of mourning. This is based on Elisabeth Kübler-Ross's characterization of how people respond to catastrophically bad news, starting with denial and ending with acceptance. In fact, bereaved people find themselves assaulted by a variety of conflicting emotions in a completely unpredictable sequence. And there are some losses that we are forced to live with but can never truly "accept."

A further false belief is that grief is something to avoid. In fact, it is unavoidable; it cannot be overcome, only experienced. The only "treatment" is to teach people to tolerate some extremely distressing emotions, including anxiety, confusion, and a wish to be dead. Commonly, those in the early stages of grief believe that they are "going crazy."

Bereaved people want to know, "How long will I be this way? What is the goal of this awful process?" The fact is that the loss of a loved one changes us permanently. There is no "closure," only softening. Dean Koontz said this in his book, *Sole Survivor:*

The few times he had gone to meetings of The Compassionate Friends, he had heard other grieving parents speak of the Zero Point. The Zero Point was the instant of the child's death, from which every future event would be dated, the eye blink during which crushing loss reset your internal gauges to zero. It was the moment at which your shabby box of hopes and wants—which had once seemed to be such a fabulous chest of bright dreams—was turned on end and emptied into an abyss, leaving you with zero expectations. In a clock tick, the future was no longer a kingdom of possibility and wonder, but a yoke of obligation—and only the unattainable past offered a hospitable place to live. He had existed at Zero Point for more than a year, with time receding from him in both directions, belonging to neither the days ahead nor those behind. It was as though he had been suspended in a tank of liquid nitrogen and lay deep in cryogenic slumber.

Another part of the cultural mythology surrounding loss is created by what I call "cheap grief." Those of us who have endured the most profound form of grief, that following the loss of a child, instantly recognize the truth of Ted Kennedy's characterization of his family's sorrow at the death of John F. Kennedy Jr. as "unspeakable." What are we to think, then, of the collective feeling abroad in the country following the death of this young man?

As with the death of Princess Diana, whatever else it was, the emotion publicly expressed after JFK Jr.'s death was eminently speakable. In fact, we were nearly drowned in words, from network anchors to pundits to people in the street appearing in front of TV cameras to say, "For me he embodied style and grace," or "I felt like he was a friend." We saw an endless repetition of the same pictures of the child and the man, shown for no other reason than to evoke some shadow of the loss that we felt at the death of his father.

In one sense there is nothing wrong with becoming emotionally involved with celebrities, including those who are famous only for being famous. Those who can't know them except through their images and through their work nevertheless feel an attachment as strong as it is unfounded in reality.

To people over fifty, Kennedy was the attractive son of a man who had once been the repository of our best hopes. To those younger he was a symbol of a culture that sanctifies youth and beauty, that cannot distinguish between celebrity and accomplishment, and that prefers its emotional experiences in the prepackaged way of television and the movies. In that sense this death was received as just another spectacle, a form of entertainment in which some of us could invest an intense and short-lived sadness.

What's wrong with this? If people want to convince themselves that something awful has happened to them in this death of a stranger, who is to say there is anything inauthentic about whatever feelings they wish to express? Well, for one thing, to those who have known real loss it looks like grief without consequences. People indulge themselves with tears, knowing that in a few days, weeks at most, they will have moved on without the lacerated heart that follows the death of someone truly central to our lives. For those who *have* borne this suffering, the public displays that accompany the death of a celebrity seem hollow. America Online reported that it was receiving one Kennedy message *per second* after this accident became known. They were, in general, all variations of "I'm deeply affected by this death." Often the sentiment was accompanied by good wishes for the families and the shallow hope that everyone would be happy soon. If consolation were the purpose of the messages, they might better have been placed in envelopes and dispatched to those who *did* know and love these people. Instead the notes read like some self-indulgent form of group therapy: We're all sad, we must be admirable.

Such "grief" is a parody of the devastation, silent and unnoticed, felt by those who have lost a child, a sibling, a young parent. Where is the endless pain, the sleepless nights, the certainty that one's life is forever diminished by random, inscrutable death?

Where is the unspeakable grief?

Loss is an inevitable consequence of the human condition. If we survive long enough we encounter many losses. The natural response to loss is grief—which looks much like depression: sadness, tears, diminished energy, changes in sleep and appetite, problems with concentration. A diminished self-esteem is more characteristic of depression. If we are grieving the loss of a loved one, we are sad, but we generally retain our sense of ourselves as worthwhile people.

What we are trying to offer any person experiencing extended or recurrent sadness is hope. Our own experiences of loss and discouragement are what we have to inform our ability to console others. The bereaved are especially sensitive to the bromides with which the uninitiated, those untouched by personal devastation, attempt to offer comfort. The grief bulletin boards of the Internet are full of the anger of people who, confronting the worst moments of their lives, are offered well-meant but ineffective attempts at consolation. Some of them—and the thoughts they evoke in grieving people—are:

- He's in a better place. (But I'm not there with him.)
- You're lucky to have other children. (I don't feel lucky.)
- I know how you feel. (Have *you* had a child die?)
- What doesn't kill us makes us stronger. (Why don't I feel stronger?)
- God doesn't give us more than we can bear. (How easy that must be to say.)
- You're so strong; I couldn't do what you have done. (What choice do I have?)
- You can get pregnant again. (So this child was disposable?)

How each of us confronts loss, in ourselves and in those we would help, defines us as few other attributes can. What we reveal in our attitudes toward grief and mourning determines whether we have anything to teach others. If we have not distilled from our own lives a sense of purpose in the face of implacable fate, how can we transmit hope to those who feel crushed by feelings of powerlessness and despair? All of us inevitably employ whatever beliefs we have, religious or philosophical, that help us to confront our mortality. Whether those we seek to help have similar convictions determines whether or not they will be useful. One need not partake of any particular doctrine, but it helps to believe in something—if only in the nobility of the human spirit in the face of the unknown.

To be mortal is to bear the awful weight of time and fate. It is in sharing this burden that we help ourselves no less than those whom we would help. We do this in an atmosphere of both pain and hope in an attempt, finally, to enable the pleasure that is also life's gift.

We all live downstream.

I t is natural to try to protect ourselves and those we love. To do this we try to construct our lives so that we are insulated from danger, both natural and man-made. In general, we build our houses above the floodplain; we immunize our children against contagious disease; we choose to live (if possible) where there is little crime; we lock our doors and install alarm systems in our houses; we insist that the government inspect the food we eat and set safety standards for the cars we drive; we fasten our seat belts, use sunblock, and avoid cigarettes; we exercise and watch our blood pressure.

In spite of all our efforts at self-protection, there is a general awareness that perfect safety is an illusion and that, in fact, our collective decision making has created a world in which we are at risk as never before. Somehow our individual needs and desires have conspired to produce a situation in which we are consuming fossil fuels at a faster rate than ever, producing deleterious effects on the air we breathe and melting the polar icecaps. Yet we go on with our lives worrying about much more improbable threats to our welfare: violent crime, mad cow disease, flu pandemics, terrorist attacks.

In a more profound sense, our shared fate in this lifeboat we call Earth depends on our stewardship of the world that is our inheritance. This is a subset of the larger truth that *it is much more difficult to create and preserve than it is to destroy.* Any eighteen-year-old can be trained in a few weeks to shoot people and blow things up efficiently. It takes a little longer to train those in the business of saving life.

We live in a world in which most of our decisions have immediate consequences. If we buy one thing we may not be able to buy another; if we have a drink now, we will feel good immediately; if we drive faster we will get there sooner; if we buy a bigger house, people will be impressed.

The focus of our thinking is conspicuously short-term. To take a longer view of our lives, to plan for retirement, for example, requires an effort many people are reluctant to make. How much harder is it, then, to ask people to contemplate the planet that their children or grandchildren will inhabit?

Most of the threats to human existence derive from a desire to bend the world to satisfy our need for rapid gratification. This, of course, is the basic philosophy of a consumer society. Look at the messages conveyed by the advertising with which we are inundated. Over and over we are presented with images of people who are clearly enjoying life more than we are. They are younger, more attractive, with more friends and an apparently inexhaustible supply of leisure time. And how can we be more like them? By spending money, of course. If we had a better car, bought some fashionable clothes, took the right antacid, lost thirty pounds, and got rid of those unsightly wrinkles, our lives would be dramatically improved.

At some level, all of us are sensible enough to know that what we have and how we look are going to keep us off the pages of *People* magazine indefinitely. Still, a chronic sense of dissatisfaction pursues us, and it is hard to live in a world in which we imagine that most other people are happier than we are. What this creates is a kind of disposable society that elevates a desire for the "new and improved" version of everything to a level of desirability that can never be satisfied. This state of mind encompasses both greed and envy; they're called *deadly* sins for a reason.

If our relentless pursuit of the latest thing is the engine that drives our consumerist culture, the by-products and side effects are worrisome and include a perceptible decline in the environment in which we must live, and ultimately in the quality of the lives we will lead.

How much more secure would we all feel if we were not dependent on foreign oil? What would our relationships with the rest of mankind be like without this need driving our foreign policy? What would each of us be willing to do (or to sacrifice) to achieve this desirable state of energy independence? These are the kinds of questions we ought to be asking instead of the ones that currently preoccupy us. At the moment we are acting like a nation driven primarily by fear. Why do the Islamists hate us? What can we do to kill or capture more of them? How much torture is OK to protect ourselves?

The connection between our insatiable consumption of the world's resources and our proclivity for using war to assert our national interests may not at first be apparent. But life teaches us over and over that *everything is connected.* This is one of the great lessons of psychotherapy: Until we put aside the rationalizations we use to protect ourselves from responsibility, we cannot grasp the essential truth that we are the same people in all areas of our lives. The guard in a concentration camp cannot exonerate himself by being a good husband and parent.

In Vietnam, soldiers were forever talking about what they would do once they returned to "the world," as if nothing they did in the war bore any relation to the rest of their lives. It was only later, in their nightmares and in their closest relationships, that they discovered the fallacy in that assumption.

So it is with a nation. We cannot consume and waste and pollute without paying a price. Similarly, we cannot bomb and torture and trample on the rights of others without compromising our sense of ourselves. People in the grip of fear do not, in general, make good decisions. This is why we need leaders to weigh the consequences of war before embarking on it. We depend on them for considered judgment and truth telling.

There is a place for violence in the world, as long as it is used only to protect ourselves and the values that make our lives worthwhile. If, however, instead of the last resort, it becomes a sort of reflex, a simple-minded reaction to our deepest dread, we put ourselves at risk no less than those we are trying to destroy. Any enterprise that is primarily destructive is unlikely to make us safer. Violence is seductive because, like most simple ideas, it appears in the short term to work. If they're dead, they can't do us harm. But what if the process of trying to kill them changes us in some fundamental way? What happens when we kill the innocent? What if the killing makes us more like those we hate? Jonathan Schell, writing about our national reaction to the *Life* magazine pictures of the My Lai massacre in Vietnam, said,

> Whether we manage to bear the grief or whether we freeze, the massacre enters into us and becomes part of us. [It] calls for self-examination and for action, but if we deny the call and try to go on as before, as though nothing had happened, our knowledge, which can never leave us once we have acquired it, will bring about an unnoticed but crucial alteration in us, numbing our most precious faculties and withering our souls. For if we learn to accept this, there is nothing we will not accept.

18

You can change who you are without rejecting who you were.

Recently I went back to West Point for my forty-fifth reunion. We members of the class of 1960 are sixty-seven years old now. We have lived through a lot: the decade of the moon landing and the war in Vietnam, the end of the cold war in which we enlisted in 1956, the advent of the Internet, and the conflicts in the desert. We're a surprisingly varied group. Only about half of us finished twenty- or thirty-year careers in the Army. The rest chose civilian vocations as businessmen, engineers, lawyers, even a poet or two. Out of the 550 of us that graduated, 82 are now dead. We lost our first classmate to an auto accident one week after graduation; our most recent death, from lung cancer, came two weeks before the reunion. In between, twelve were killed in Vietnam. We are, as expected, dying more rapidly now.

It was good to go back to that citadel of our youth and strength for the first time in many years. It looks much the same. The Gothic granite barracks have been expanded to accommodate more cadets; the Protestant chapel still dominates on the hillside. There are new buildings, and the football stadium has been improved even as the team has grown worse. On parade, the Corps of Cadets still looks to be the best close-order drill unit in the world, though the sight of women marching, even leading companies and battalions, is difficult to absorb for older graduates, steeped in the monastic masculinity of outdated tradition.

The real evidence that the place has changed, however, came on Friday night, when the entertainment in Eisenhower Hall consisted of Jon Stewart doing a stand-up routine in front of hundreds of cadets. They loved him.

The History Department is compiling oral histories from graduates who have served in combat, apparently in an effort to impart to the cadets of today some lessons that they can use in wars of the future. This is how I came to be interviewed by an earnest young major about my experiences as the Regimental Surgeon of the 11th Armored Cavalry Regiment in Vietnam. He sent me some questions ahead of time ("How can current cadets best prepare for their roles as officers in an unconventional environment?"). I wanted to talk about something else: What does a soldier do when he discovers that the rationale for the war he has been sent to fight bears no relationship to what is happening on the ground?

What I found in Vietnam was that in spite of our protestations about "winning hearts and minds," we treated the Vietnamese with contempt. They were commonly called "gooks" and "dinks." As a doctor I was required to provide medical care to wounded prisoners who were tortured during questioning. I was asked by the regimental intelligence officer if I would administer succinyl choline to temporarily paralyze the muscles of respiration of POWs as an aid to interrogation. I could not abide it, and after six months I registered a public protest during a change-of-command ceremony for my commanding officer. I was arrested for "conduct unbecoming an officer," and my career in military medicine was over.

It was the first time since I returned from Vietnam thirty-six years ago that West Point had shown an interest in what happened to me there. So into that video camera I poured everything I could say in an hour about what I had seen and done and learned. I didn't have much advice to offer cadets.

I just told my story and asked them to think about who they are and where their core identities fit with their duty as soldiers, what they stand for and what they cannot. I have no idea whether any cadet will ever see this tape, but it was an important moment for me nonetheless. It was the confession of a man once faced with an irresolvable conflict between my loyalty to the Army and my deepest convictions about what it means to be a physician, a patriotic American, and a free man upon the earth.

And through it all ran my love for West Point, which had brought me back one more time to celebrate my connection with the place that had taught me the values of honor and obligation that I tried to reify, even at the cost of all that I had aspired to be.

On the afternoon I left home for my reunion, I received an e-mail from the mother of a young West Point graduate recently killed in South Asia. She had read a book of mine and wanted something that might comfort her in her mourning. I sent her a prayer I had composed for bereaved parents after the death of my six-year-old son:

May we all find peace in the shared hope that our children who brought us such joy with their short lives are now a host of angels, loving us still, feeling our love for them, awaiting our coming, and knowing that they are safely locked forever in our hearts.

During our reunion we had a memorial service for our departed classmates in which each of their names was called out by someone who had been his friend. We prayed for their eternal rest and sang the alma mater. We listened to a retired general evoke their memories with clichés about honor and duty and freedom that are as inevitable as they are irrelevant to men who died in ways heroic and prosaic, with thoughts and fears likely unrelated to the mantle of patriotism in which we would now wrap their souls.

In the chapel at West Point, as before the black granite wall in Washington, I remember my classmates dead in Vietnam, eternally young, immortal in my mortal mind. They will not grow old and frail like the rest of us. They will not linger on beds of pain. Perhaps, after all, they are the lucky ones. But what of the songs unsung, the children and grandchildren unborn, the peaceful pleasures of long-time love? These things they were denied.

The circle, it seems, is never closed. I fear that young men and women are still dying for reasons that forty-five years from now will cause another group of old graduates to honor their memories, as did we, with devotion and regret.

It is a sense of meaning that nourishes the soul.

Of all the reasons we work, the effort to leave a footprint to mark our passing on the earth is the most compelling. Among those who come to me with their stories, it is easy to get caught up in the medical cycle of diagnosis and treatment. It is not hard to recognize depression and anxiety, the two most common disorders of those who seek help from a psychiatrist. The fact that we now have medications that are effective in lifting these burdens from people can obscure the fact that happiness is much more than the absence of depression.

I often tell people that the medicine I am about to give them is designed only to relieve the burden of depression: the crushing weight, the cloud, the shackles that rob their lives of pleasure, their nights of sleep, and their closest relationships of the simple joys of companionship and intimacy. For many people, this is more than enough help. Relief from a pain long endured is a state devoutly to be wished, and people are grateful. For many, it is like being freed from prison, though the important question remains: free to do what?

And yet, pleasure is not the absence of pain, nor is health the absence of disease. It is what we do and who we are with that makes us happy. In a larger sense, our mortality confronts us with questions of meaning. What is the point of our daily struggles? Most of us now have the leisure to contemplate the reasons driving our work and our play.

There is a certain emptiness to the simple equation of work and consumption. ("I shop, therefore I am.") None of us are young enough or rich enough to live up to the icons we create to stoke the engines of commerce. No one is immune to these influences, but all of us are in danger of endorsing the superficiality they purvey. The pictures of people in stores trampling each other to get to bargains on the aptly named "Black Friday" after Thanksgiving are both revealing and disturbing.

In our daily lives, questions of personal worth are recurrent, if seldom articulated. This is never more evident than in the lives of those who retire. We are so defined by our work that our identities without it are in question. Unless we have something else to anchor us, we are in danger of disappearing, of becoming unseen by those who are still "productive." Our families provide the most obvious continuing connections to a meaningful life. In this society, however, the status of the elderly is sufficiently devalued that even family ties are freighted with questions of mental and physical decline.

The groundwork for this unenviable state has been laid in the choices we make when young. The nature of most work—repetitive and unsatisfying—guarantees that we think of our jobs as little more than a means to support ourselves and to enable us to pursue leisure activities that commonly add little to our sense of personal significance. We are, in short, starved for meaning.

I am convinced that this vacuum is what accounts for our fondness for organized religion. Deprived of a clear sense of purpose or satisfaction, apprehensive about the significance of our lives, fearful of the apparent finality of death, we are desperate for an explanation for our existence and eager for some reassurance that there is a guiding purpose behind our daily struggles. By agreeing to a set of divinely inspired rules, required only to come together regularly with like-minded believers to affirm our faith, we gain reassurance that we are not alone in the face of the great mysteries of life and death, and that however unhappy life makes us, there is salvation at the end.

But religious belief is not the only path to a life of meaning. It is possible to revere our world and the people in it, to accept the uncertainty that is the hallmark of our world, and to place one's faith in the angels of our better nature. Above all, we might do well to cultivate a certain humility about our particular conception of what constitutes an ethical life and be willing to accept those who peacefully disagree with us. If we can save our own souls, whatever that might mean to each of us, we will have succeeded mightily.

We were not meant to live alone.

F ewer than half of American households contain married couples. Obviously, many people are in living arrangements that are "nontraditional." For some this is a temporary situation while they seek someone to whom to attach themselves. Others, presumably, are single by choice.

Most of the attention given to people who are single goes to those in their twenties and thirties. They are the ones celebrated in popular entertainment: delaying marriage and engaging in the "tribal pleasures" afforded by their close friendships. There doesn't appear to be much that is considered glamorous about the people I see most frequently, trying in middle age to cope with the unwanted and unfamiliar status of being single after failed marriages of long duration.

Whether one is left or does the leaving, the breakdown of a relationship in which one has invested much hope and many years is a daunting experience. The fact that it may be financially catastrophic and complicate the raising of children only deepens the emotional loss and accounts for the fact that many people elect to remain in unhappy marriages.

We are so socialized to see the universe as consisting of people who have paired off that not to be part of a couple carries a social stigma. Single people past a certain age commonly feel devalued. They tend to cluster in organizations whose primary purpose is to find a mate. Forty million Americans now visit online dating services, and the Internet personals market is a $500 million business. Innovations like "speed dating," "silent dating," and "dating in the dark" also serve as shortcuts for those who lack the time or patience for more traditional ways of meeting people. Reality TV has portrayed the process of finding someone to love as the emotional equivalent of a contact sport.

Those more determinedly single can join groups that promote an image of empowerment like quirkyalone.net or the aggressively named leatherspinsters.com. What is being advocated by these groups is the idea that people can live happy single lives without being defined by "the tyranny of coupledom." What appears to be necessary to do this is a social network of like-minded people.

At issue in all these efforts is the nature of happiness and the conditions necessary for it. Of all the requirements people set—financial security, meaningful work, satisfying leisure, friendships—the one most assiduously sought is long-term intimacy with another human being, usually, though not necessarily, of the opposite sex. Based as it is on our animal instinct to reproduce, satisfaction of this drive transcends all others not directly related to physical survival.

Even at points in our lives when reproduction is no longer desired or even possible, the psychological need for intimate companionship retains its power. Few of us can be happily alone for extended periods. Those who can be usually require some powerful alternative source of significance, such as religious faith or the pursuit of some challenge of exploration or adventure.

Most of us need to love and be loved, more or less continuously. Deprived of this experience, we tend to become discouraged and bitter. People who have been widowed can retain over many years the sense of love and commitment to the lost spouse. Though no longer visibly part of a couple, they may move beyond their grief to live happily with their memories and their hopes of reunion. It is hard to have a similar experience after divorce, when feelings of failure and resentment are more the norm. It is sometimes *not* better to have loved and lost.

However we may try to deny it ("We're single and proud!"), there are few among us who do not want to be part of a couple. We may be able to function well, work productively, and have satisfying friendships as a single person, but it is more than social pressures and anxious parents that pushes us at all stages of life to seek the cherished other.

This longing is more than a need for companionship. We have a need to see ourselves reflected in the eyes of someone who regards us as an indispensable part of his or her life. What we seek (and seldom find) is unconditional love. There has been a lot of discussion about whether this is an unreasonable demand to place on an adult who did not give birth to us. Frequently, we are required to settle for less, sometimes much less. Most intimate relationships, especially those of long standing, have a contractual quality and appear to be more or less friendly, unwritten agreements between people who consent to perform reciprocal services.

Traditionally, this arrangement was obvious, with the man providing income and the woman expected to contribute domestic and child-rearing services. In return, both parties obtained access to companionship, including regular (if unexciting) sex, in an economically viable pair-bond that provided a stable environment in which to raise children and thereby satisfy the need to meet our own and society's expectations.

With the availability of reliable contraception and the greater economic independence of women, who often chose to delay childbearing while they pursued careers, things started breaking down on the marital front. Men became expected to do some housework and share decision-making power with women who were no longer financially trapped in their marriages. As divorce became easier and less stigmatizing, we saw more of it as both men and women came to see no point in living indefinitely with people they no longer liked or respected. The irony of these developments is that instead of a big increase of singles, we simply had more people in second and third marriages.

A lot of seemingly good ideas from the 1960s never worked out: communal living that was supposed to abolish jealousy, for instance. And formal marriage contracts that specified each party's responsibilities. And promises to stay with the other person "as long as we both shall love." You don't hear that much anymore, even from those who write their own vows. Apparently, people prefer to make enduring promises that only half of them ultimately keep.

It does no good to maintain that things should be different. That we should all be content to be with ourselves, having lots of friendships and as much casual sex as we need without encumbering relationships with the burden of marriage. Logic has little to do with this demonstrated desire for one other person who will promise with a straight face to love us forever. If it doesn't last quite that long, at least we will have felt "normal" for a little while. And then we can always try again.

The primary difference between intelligence and stupidity is that there are limits to intelligence.

P eople tend to put a lot of stock in the ability of human beings to reason. We think it's what makes us special among the creatures of the earth. So why does so much of our national discourse sound like the debating society of a confederacy of dunces?

Consider the long-running dispute over the public display of the Ten Commandments. It strains credulity to pretend that the conflict between the Christian fundamentalists and the rest of us is somehow a legitimate constitutional debate over issues like freedom of religious expression and the establishment clause of the First Amendment.

Let's take the monument worshipers first. (A better example of a "golden calf" would be hard to find. Where is Moses when we need him?) My fellow West Point graduate and chief justice of the Alabama Supreme Court, Roy Moore, had the 5,300-pound representation of the Ten Commandments placed in the lobby of the Judicial Building in Montgomery several years ago. (Currently, it's touring the country on a flatbed truck.) He has subsequently said that the commandments are "the moral foundation of American law." It would be hard to construct a sillier rationalization than that.

Seven of the ten commandments bear little relation to American law. Except for the prohibitions against killing, stealing, and bearing false witness, we are left only with warnings about swearing, graven images, coveting, adultery, and honoring our parents. None of the latter has been the subject of contemporary legislation. For Christians (and Jews), of course, the big #1 is: "I am the Lord thy God. Thou shalt have no other gods before me." For Muslims, this translates as "There is no God but Allah and Mohammed is his prophet." Take your pick. To a true believer of any of those faiths, you either accept the commandment or you are lost.

Throughout the civil rights movement, the faith of the

protesters and their leaders gave them the courage and moral certainty to confront the forces of segregation, many of whom, like the Ku Klux Klan, invoked their own version of Christianity to justify their resistance to the struggle for racial equality.

The people who assembled in Montgomery to resist the removal of the Ten Commandments monument are the spiritual descendants of the segregationists, as shown by the presence of the Confederate battle flag among them. Unlike the inclusive, nonviolent, and forgiving beliefs that inspired the civil rights marchers, the faith of the fundamentalists is coercive, exclusive, and of a piece with the stance taken by that other Alabama hero of 1963, Governor George Wallace, who incited the resistance of citizens to federal authority by "standing in the schoolhouse door" to oppose the desegregation of the state university.

An ostensible pillar of conservative belief is the enforcement of restrictions on government interference in people's lives. However, as with the Ten Commandments, fundamentalist conservatives are eager to force their social views on the rest of us, usually on moral and religious grounds. In fact, it is their insistence on a particular interpretation of the Bible that makes some of them sound like the theocrats of Iran. They are heedless of contradictions in their beliefs. For example, they are firmly against the taking of unborn life while supporting strict enforcement (and extensions) of the death penalty.

The important thing to recognize, I think, is that political beliefs exist not just on a continuum but on a sort of circle where the extremists at either end are more like each other than they are like those in the middle. The extreme of conservatism would be fascism, that of liberal thinking, communism. Hitler and Stalin—theoretically at opposite ends of the political spectrum—both created totalitarian states that murdered millions. The genius of the American system of government is that, over 220 years, it has acted as a sort of political gyroscope that has avoided the extremes and kept us all free to live our lives, and—with the exception of the Civil War—to disagree with each other without bloodshed. In many ways, the important debate going on in this country is not between liberals and conservatives but between extremists and moderates.

A 2004 Harris poll on religion is instructive. An unsurprising 90 percent of adult Americans profess a belief in God. What is more interesting is that half believe in ghosts, almost a third believe in astrology, and more than a quarter believe that they themselves were reincarnated from other people. Two-thirds believe in the devil and hell (but hardly anyone expects that they will go there themselves). Another survey disclosed that Americans are three times as likely to believe in the virgin birth of Jesus (83 percent) as in evolution (28 percent).

Ah, yes. Evolution. Unable to accept a scientific theory so at odds with a literal interpretation of the Bible, creationists have now come up with an alternative explanation: intelligent design, the idea that an organism's complexity is evidence of the existence of a cosmic designer. Against the sheer amount of physical evidence that Charles Darwin was right is arrayed a biblical story that cannot be tested scientifically and is therefore not a "theory" in any scientific sense. There is no experiment or collection of evidence that would show that the idea of intelligent design is not true. It rests simply on faith. That the president would advocate its teaching in science classes alongside evolution "so people can understand what the debate is about" is a striking example of ignorance in action.

It would be wrong to tar all conservative thinkers with the same brush. It is obviously possible for people of good will and intelligence to disagree politically. It is at the edges of any philosophy that one encounters those who are so sure they are right that they believe they must convert or compel those who disagree with them. The engine that drives this impulse to dominate is often religious. It requires the certainty of the true believer to justify the forcible imposition of one's view of the world.

The primary difference between intelligence and stupidity is that there are limits to intelligence.

Of all the rights guaranteed us by our Constitution and laws, the one that is seldom discussed but universally enjoyed is the right to be left alone. The exercise of this entitlement requires not just freedom *of* religion, but also freedom *from* religion. Is it not warning enough that the fundamentalists have produced a president who has taken us upon a "crusade" against the "evildoers"—who, unsurprisingly, turn out to be fundamentalists of a different stripe?

The reconciliation of these tensions in American society, between the religious conservatives who currently control the levers of government and those who welcome a more tolerant, pluralistic nation, will be a long process. Yet there are hopeful signs that the pendulum is moving away from the extremism that has so dominated the national dialogue over the past six years. The catastrophe in Iraq, the economic injustice of corporate looters, the effort to transfer more wealth to the wealthy by using the tax code, a disdain for civil liberties, a lack of respect for the opinions of the rest of the world, the governmental incompetence and social inequities laid bare by the hurricanes have all combined to produce a kind of national revulsion against a philosophy that appears to embody so much selfishness, intolerance, and death. If the pendulum is indeed moving, it will not be a moment too soon.

22

The ears are the primary organs of seduction.

I am confronted daily with the difficulty people have in thinking systematically, in recognizing that life is to a large extent an exercise in trial-and-error learning. Parents who spank their children as a means of discipline are puzzled by the intractability of the child's oppositional behavior. Wedded to the idea (usually taught them by their own parents) that pain and intimidation are useful tools for controlling unwanted behavior, they ignore evidence that the incongruity between what they seek to teach the child (politeness and tractability) and the method they use (violence) is at the root of the child's confusion and resentment. The question that I frequently ask: "Is that working?" is often one that parents have failed to ask themselves.

Pragmatic, evidence-based, "logical" approaches to problem solving, particularly in the areas of human relationships, are unusual. More often we behave as we do out of long-established habit. To change requires more than new knowledge. There must also be an emotional commitment. Frustration, anger, discouragement, anxiety, even despair are all feelings that can cause people to examine their lives, and particularly their closest relationships. The hope of resolving these emotions constitutes the primary incentive for change. The therapist's role is to provide insight and encouragement in the difficult task of translating new knowledge into changed behavior.

To that end, the first task in therapy is to establish trust. Apart from the socially sanctioned role of helper, the therapist is often placed in other roles, including confessor, teacher, parent, and judge. People's preconceptions about therapy are born of years of watching depictions of the process on television and in the movies. Psychiatrists are frequently portrayed as criminals (Hannibal Lecter in *The Silence of the Lambs* comes to mind) or as laughably disturbed (Mel Brooks as Dr. Richard Thorndyke in *High Anxiety*). Radio and TV therapists, in their efforts to be entertaining, present an image of shoot-from-the-hip advice giving that skews patients' expectations.

Why should one person pay another for conversation? This essential question hangs over any first contact with a patient. Because there has been a gradual destigmatization of the need to seek emotional help, aided by the efficacy of anti-anxiety/antidepressant medicines developed over the last fifty years, people are more willing to entertain the possibility that their lives might be improved if they understood them better. Still, it often requires a long period of emotional discomfort before someone is ready to come for help.

The first thing I wonder when meeting a new patient is, "What is this person's readiness for change?" People frequently consult a psychiatrist at the behest of others, usually members of their family, who find their behavior troubling. Wives threatening divorce, parents at their wits' end, angry bosses or coworkers, all can serve as incentives to seek help. But without a decision on the part of the person himself that the time has come for new behavior, the process of therapy is likely to be unavailing.

My first impulse on meeting someone new is to listen, with as few interruptions as possible, to what they have to say. This may seem obvious, but in the era of managed care, with people typically seen for medication evaluations every fifteen minutes, there is little incentive for uninterrupted listening.

It was surprising to me to learn a long time ago what a powerful instrument of change listening is. I think that this is because people in general are starved for the experience of being heard. Most of our entertainment requires only passive participation—in effect, listening to others. Our politicians talk at us as if they were the source of all useful knowledge. Even those we are closest to are frequently so busy they don't have the time (or interest) to engage in quiet conversation. In this atmosphere, the experience of being listened to is, for many, an unusual and satisfying experience. Each of our stories deserves to be told, and yet to whom can we tell them?

The act of listening has the effect of establishing and reaffirming our concern about the other person. A standard complaint that women (who tend to be better listeners and therefore have more friends than men) have about their spouses is a failure to listen, that is, pay attention. Like most cultural clichés, this one has a lot of truth to it. Men are socialized to compete, and in spite of the gender enlightenment of recent decades, they are still hesitant to reveal, especially to each other, anything that might be construed as weakness. I have run a men's therapy group for thirty years, and the process of men seeking help from each other and the changed dynamic produced by the absence of women in the room has been fascinating to observe. All the qualities that isolate men from other people and their own feelings have been on display: competitiveness, a fetish for self-sufficiency, and a striking inability even to give a name to emotions.

The technical term for this trouble with labeling what one feels is "alexithymia." It suggests a distancing mechanism that prevents people from acknowledging, hence experiencing, discordant emotions. If one has no ability to use words like anger, joy, fear, or love, it is very difficult to understand or converse about one's inner life. If it is true that the Inuit have thirty words for snow and none for war, it suggests something more than that they live in cold places.

When trying to help people change, it is important for a therapist to have what I call "leverage." When meeting a therapist for the first time, it is difficult to have much confidence that he or she can do anything useful for us. Even with whatever social sanction comes with diplomas on the wall and a listing in the yellow pages, the therapist is still a stranger of whom one is naturally skeptical. It is only through the establishment of a relationship and some demonstration of interest and competence to understand that people will begin both to reveal themselves and to listen to what the therapist has to say. Most of all, patients *must* have the clear sense that they are not being judged and that the therapist is on their side.

It is a commentary on our close relationships that it is so unclear to many whether their spouses are supporters or adversaries. The pervasive acceptance of the idea that all married people fight is a product of an unspoken belief that marriage implies a kind of power struggle in which partners need to learn to negotiate differences and "fight fair." The idea that the other person is a source of reliable support who sees your interests as equal to his or her own is commonly regarded as a naïve belief.

We live in a society dedicated to winning. In sports, politics, business, and in our ways of relating to each other, we are encouraged to think in terms of a competitive model. This simplistic approach, winning or losing, may work for football, but it ignores the fact that most of our decisions and outcomes emerge from myriad possibilities. Failure to grasp this results in people selecting a course of action because the only alternative they can visualize is its opposite. For example, asking a rigid and punitive parent to examine his or her behavior often produces the question, "What do you suggest, letting the kid do whatever he wants?"

This two-alternatives, win/lose, black/white thinking ignores the subtleties and shades of gray that characterize the real world and inhibits our ability to function successfully within it. This is also why the process of therapy lacks the clarity and precision that is such a satisfying part of popular entertainment. Most human conflict is full of uncertainty and ambiguity. To resolve differences, therefore, requires an ability to acknowledge this, to see things from the other person's point of view, and to give up the satisfaction of being "right." Not everyone can do this, which is why so many find it hard to sustain relationships.

Another untoward side effect of popular culture is a short-ening of attention span. Apart from our fondness for the remote control, we have grown accustomed to seeing com-plicated and conflicted situations resolved in an hour or two. We grow bored and impatient with the maddeningly slow pace of real-life conflict resolution. Images of quick success and instant wealth are all around us. The slow process of building things, especially relationships, that endure seems vaguely old-fashioned. Glitz, glamour, and ephemeral beauty capture our interest and tantalize our imaginations. We are changed by these images in our magazines and on our TV screens. They serve as sources of dissatisfaction and longing that contrast with the relatively less exciting reality of our daily lives.

So we pay attention to movie stars, buy lottery tickets, sue each other, and grow impatient with our partners—all expressions of discontent with what we have and what we are. Is it any wonder, then, that we are limited in what we have to give to and expect from each other, and unsuited to the task of building and sustaining relationships? These attitudes also inhibit any process of change, no matter how much we purport to want it. Because our desires are so powerful for what we cannot have—wealth, beauty, and unlimited happiness—we find it difficult to think logically about how to achieve the more prosaic but longer-lasting satisfactions that *are* available to us.

People can concentrate on only one idea at a time. If we are preoccupied with superficialities, we are unlikely to reflect on what is important. If we value entertainment over enlightenment, we sacrifice our only chance at a real understanding of what works. We are thereby prevented from modifying our behavior in response to experience, which is the very definition of learning. If we cannot learn, we become little more than a collection of unexamined habits, subject to the mindless repetition of past mistakes. Does this sound like a prescription for happiness?

No one ever died of insomnia.

Difficulty sleeping is a frequent complaint of people seeking psychiatric care. Sometimes it's the only complaint: "If I could just get a good night's sleep, everything would be fine." Because insomnia is a frequent symptom of both anxiety and depression, it would seem to make sense to attack it by treating the underlying problem. I tend to regard sleeplessness as a "teachable moment" and encourage patients to reflect on their lives in an effort to discover what may be causing the problem. This approach flies in the face of the immediate relief that people have been led to expect by the drug companies that make sleep medicines.

I went to a psychiatric meeting recently at one of our area's finest restaurants (sponsored, of course, by a pharmaceutical company) in which the topic was insomnia. As my fellow psychiatrists discussed their approaches to the problem, the emphasis was solely on which medication they preferred. When I suggested that I usually direct patients' attention to what might be causing their sleep problems rather than starting them immediately on habit-forming drugs, people looked at me as if I had suggested a seventeenth-century remedy—bleeding, or leeches perhaps. It was apparent that giving drugs to put people to sleep was simply the most cost-effective approach. It worked, met patient expectations, and allowed one to quickly move on to the next person on the schedule. It was not hard to see why the drug company had found it cost-effective to buy us the meal we had just consumed.

Here's the paradox of sleep: *You can't have it until it's not important to you.* Since it is an involuntary activity, it can't be forced. This, of course, is infinitely annoying to those who have been taught that everything yields to hard work, and for whom control is a big issue in their lives. In fact, the harder you try to sleep, the more elusive it is. So the usual strategy of insomniacs—lying in bed watching the clock and thinking about how tired they are going to be in the morning—virtually guarantees that they will remain awake.

When patients demand an immediate solution to the problem, I tell them about the paradox and suggest that they deemphasize the importance of sleep as a way of making it more likely to occur. We have all been sold a bill of goods about the importance of sleep. Like consulting your doctor before exercise, getting an annual physical exam, avoiding drafts in winter, and not swimming after eating, the importance of a solid eight hours of sleep a night is a myth. In fact, most people can function well on a lot less, *and* our bodies can be trusted to make up sleep deficits before we collapse from fatigue.

The purveyors and prescribers of sleep medication are constantly warning us that insomnia is a dangerous epidemic in the society, the cause of frequent fatal auto accidents and a plague on the productivity of American students and workers. A recent newspaper article warned that the latest scientific research suggested that "failing to get enough sleep or sleeping at odd hours heightens the risk of a variety of major illnesses, including cancer, heart disease, diabetes, and obesity." No wonder people are worried and sleepless. As with most other forms of anxiety, insomnia feeds on itself. Whatever it was that initially made us anxious, we are now anxious about being anxious, afraid of being afraid. Now there's *no* chance that we will sleep, short of utter exhaustion or general anesthesia (which I occasionally recommend to those whose preoccupation with sleep is intractable).

So here is what I tell people: (1) insomnia isn't a very interesting topic for discussion; (2) your body can be trusted to ensure that you get enough sleep to prevent you from collapsing; and (3) you won't be able to sleep until sleeping becomes unimportant to you. The best way to diminish the importance of sleep is not to remain in bed awake longer than thirty minutes at a time. If you're not asleep by then, get up and do something useful—read, work, scrub the kitchen floor. Stay up for at least forty-five minutes before going back to bed. Repeat this cycle as necessary. The theory, of course, is that instead of lying in bed in a state of sleep-preventing anxiety, one is presenting one's body with two good alternatives: sleep or some other constructive activity. This lowers anxiety and, in most cases, results in improved sleep. Meanwhile, I require people to limit discussion of their sleep problems to no more than five minutes of each therapy session. This not only avoids boredom on my part but insures that we have time to talk about more important issues.

Whether our lives are happy or sad, satisfying or not, is, in large measure, determined by what we choose to pay attention to. For those who find life discouraging and the world a dangerous place, full of venality and misery, there is no shortage of supporting evidence. The pages of our daily newspapers are virtually an unbroken chronicle of death, destruction, and the worst that human nature has to offer. Some people get so caught up in their consumption of such "news" that it affects their moods and their outlook on life. Most of what we fear is a reaction to what we see on our television screens.

Just as pessimists turn out to be right in the long run, so those who see the world through the filter provided by a medium whose motto for TV news is "If it bleeds, it leads" are likely to have their cynical and fearful views of the world confirmed. Conversely, if we spend as much time as possible in the presence of beauty and generosity, we are likely to think of ourselves as fortunate and of other people as well intentioned.

The same thing, interestingly, applies to the way we regard our physical and mental health. If we are convinced by exposure to media portrayals that we are in danger of contracting mad cow disease, we may deny ourselves the pleasures of eating steak. (My apologies to the vegetarians among us, who doubtless deserve to outlive the rest of us.) Because planes crash, albeit infrequently, some people travel no farther than their cars will take them. Those with some rudimentary understanding of statistics are able to eat better and journey to distant places.

By the same token, if we have confidence in our bodies and minds to heal and protect themselves, we can avoid a lot of unnecessary trips to the doctor. If one walks into a hospital emergency room at any time of day, one will see a waiting room full of people with self-limited conditions that are causing temporary discomfort and require no treatment. These people, "the worried well," are willing to wait hours to see an over-worked physician who, in most cases, either has no idea what is wrong with them or has little to offer in the way of real treat-ment. People come for help under these conditions because they are afraid that their symptoms are an indication of a serious problem ("I have a cough, I wonder if it could be SARS") or because they are intolerant of discomfort ("Don't you have *something* that will take this headache away?"). The fact is that there are entire industries that depend on people's per-ception that there is a diagnosis for every constellation of symptoms (e.g., fibromyalgia, chronic fatigue syndrome, sleep apnea) and a pill for every pain. The medical-care system itself reinforces hypochondriacal behavior ("Just to be safe, I'm going to run a few tests"). Even the "holistic health" move-ment with its stores full of "natural remedies" encourages the view that we need to be alert for such things as "sick-building syndrome" and heavy-metal poisoning.

Enough. We are wonderfully made and our bodies are miracles of regeneration and self-healing. Have a little confidence. The less you're around doctors, the better you're likely to feel. If you're having trouble sleeping, learn to enjoy the peace and quiet of the early morning hours when the phone is not ringing and no one is sending you e-mail. Read that book you've been meaning to get to and trust your body to go to sleep when it's tired enough. If that doesn't work and you can't stand another night awake, type "insomnia" into the search engine of your computer. In no time you'll be on a listserv with a whole new group of friends.

Heroism is in the eye of the beholder.

Some words in the English language have been rendered meaningless or obsolete by overuse. *Awesome*, for example, has been vandalized into oblivion by teenagers and by adults trying to talk like teenagers. A perfectly good adverb, *hopefully*, has been transformed (primarily by interviews with athletes) into a three-syllable substitute for *I hope*. *Utilize* has become a pretentious replacement for *use*. Cop talk has caused us to refer to people by the distancing designation of *individuals* ("The individual exited the vehicle" sounds so much more official than "The man got out of the car"). We have been numbed by computerspeak (input, output, interface). Nouns have become verbs simply by osmosis (impact, access, host) or through the use of -*ize* (finalize, maximize, strategize, prioritize). Even as I type this my computer spellcheck accepts these usages as legitimate words, thereby legitimizing them.

But of all the degradation of language that we have had to accept, the loss of meaning of the word *hero* is perhaps the most regrettable. Now practically everyone who dies with a uniform on is so designated. One of the things one quickly learns in combat is that who gets shot or blown up is seldom correlated with the courage they exhibited. As a matter of fact, death on the battlefield is almost exclusively a matter of luck. This is especially true in our current war, where most of the casualties are inflicted by roadside bombs. Which vehicle you happen to be riding in determines whether you live or die.

Obviously, there are people who do courageous things in war and this is what the military system of valor awards is designed to recognize (though, even here, dying usually ensures some sort of medal). Simply getting killed, however, doesn't qualify in my mind as heroism. What's missing is the element of choice. Now, it can be argued that taking the risk of being in a volunteer army at war is choice enough, but how about all those reservists and National Guardsmen and women who sign up for one thing (college benefits, humanitarian service, two weeks a year of active duty) and get something entirely different—exposure to actual combat? If we denied heroic status to those struck down by random bullets, or blown up while driving down the road, we would be left with a much smaller cohort of people who died bravely while taking exceptional risks. Maybe CBS could rename its "fallen heroes" segment on the national news "unlucky soldiers." It's truer, but it doesn't have quite the same ring to it.

Some years ago several American airmen were briefly detained in China after a collision between their spy plane and an aggressive Chinese fighter aircraft. Their repatriation was scripted to evoke memories of the arrival of the POWs at the end of the Vietnam War—right down to family members rushing into the arms of the returned airmen. (Were we supposed to think, "My God, these men haven't seen their children for . . . two weeks?")

On August 30, 2002, Newark International Airport was renamed Newark Liberty "to honor defenders of freedom and the heroes of September 11." While there were doubtless heroes (mostly unknown) that day, nearly all of the 3,000 victims of the attacks were simply extremely unlucky. They were stock brokers, secretaries, maintenance people, restaurant employees, and others who simply showed up for work. Again, they did not choose to put themselves in jeopardy and so fail this crucial test for heroism. (And did their families deserve all that money, an average of $3.1 million? Why not do the same for the equally unlucky families who lost relatives in the Oklahoma City bombing, or in hurricanes and other natural disasters?)

How about the 460 firemen and policemen who died trying to save civilians? The choice to take on this work represents an acknowledgment of its risks. Those who do so are, in general, brave people to be willing to protect and save the rest of us if necessary. But when a building unexpectedly falls on you, you are no more or less brave than those who, completely randomly, escaped. When complimented for heroism, most firemen and police officers respond, "I was just doing my job." It sounds modest, but it is usually the truth.

Some years ago a pilot crash-landed an airliner with frozen controls that could only be steered using differential power in the engines on each wing. His skill saved two-thirds of the passengers on board. Heroic? Nope (as he has repeatedly affirmed). Again, he didn't choose to be in that situation. He simply coped with adversity exceptionally well.

So, choice and risk, preferably on behalf of others, are the crucial elements of heroism. Death alone is not enough. Looking for heroes? How about the passengers on United flight 93? Confronted with terrorists with knives, they organized themselves and rushed the cockpit. Could any of us have behaved as well? I don't know if I could. That's what makes them heroes for me. (Why didn't their families get a "bravery bonus?")

And what about people who display exceptional courage over a period of years rather than minutes? Like Senator John McCain, who as a prisoner of war in Vietnam declined early release to stand by his fellow captives. Parents of sick and disabled children routinely exhibit a level of commitment and unselfishness that is both breathtaking and unrecognized. Those struggling with the loss of loved ones or facing their own mortality with grace and generosity deserve, but seldom receive, our admiration. In fact, they are virtually invisible in our celebrity-fixated culture. This is ironic, since, life being what it is, all of us eventually will have our chance to be brave—or not.

Why is any of this important? Why not confer hero status posthumously on every soldier unlucky enough to die? Surely, his or her family appreciates it. But more is at stake here than cheapening the language. We have always looked to heroes as examples for the rest of us. We would like to imagine that we would behave well in dangerous situations, that we would have it within us to overcome our fear and self-interest enough to help others. Of course, we can never know in advance how we would react to a life-threatening crisis, but if we hope to do so courageously, we need examples of genuine heroes to give us models for good behavior. We cannot get this from the actors or athletes who are routinely the objects of our adulation. We are in desperate need of the real thing, so we ought to be careful who we choose.

We are all capable of anything.

I was raised in upstate New York. My father was fond of guns. He gave me my first rifle when I was seven years old, a bolt-action, .22 caliber Mossberg. I spent many hours alone in the woods with that weapon. At first I fired only at tin cans on fence posts. Later I moved on to small animals, squirrels and woodchucks mostly. I became used to the sight of blood and, like many of my friends, I aspired to be a cowboy or a soldier, a hunter of men. My father, whom I sought to please, was proud of my marksmanship. Guns were symbols of power, control, masculinity—all the things a young boy longs for and lacks.

Once, when I was eleven, my father and I were planting pine trees on a hillside of our farm. I had brought my rifle with me in case a bobcat appeared, as one had while my mother was working in one of our apple orchards a few weeks earlier. It was a hot day. We had been putting the seedlings in the earth for hours, and I was exhausted from the rhythm of turning the sod and planting the small trees on the rocky, uneven slope—row after row at six-foot intervals. My father, who never seemed to tire, was shirtless, and I watched the sweat run down his muscular back.

We spoke hardly at all as we worked, and I felt that there was no escaping the mindless labor until all the seedlings were in the ground. My father would have let me go back to the house and its coolness, but to be outworked by a man forty years older was a humiliation that I was unprepared to accept. Taking a break, I walked to where my rifle lay in the hot grass and sat down beside it. With no conscious thought I picked up the weapon and casually sighted on a tree at the edge of the field.

Slowly, as in a dream, I felt the rifle swinging until it was pointed at my father's back, thirty feet away, bent to plant yet another pine. My finger was on the trigger and I snapped off the safety. How long were we like that, a tableau of the love and hate and rivalry that passes between fathers and sons? I can remember feeling only a sense of power that, in later years, I came to regard as a kind of insanity. Perhaps there was no chance that I could have pulled that trigger. But in my trance, in the breezeless heat of the late-morning sun, amid the sound of grasshoppers, I felt only the emptiness of a summer with no end, no pleasure, and no meaning.

If, in that moment, my father had turned around, I thought that an awful secret would have been revealed and both our lives might have ended on that hill in a kind of primitive sacrifice beyond morality or explanation.

Gradually, seemingly of its own accord, the muzzle lowered. I snapped the safety on and replaced the rifle in the grass. My father turned and dropped his spade to the ground.

"What do you say, pal? How about some lunch?"

"Sounds good, Dad."

26

We are drowning in information but starved for knowledge.

When we contemplate what we "know," how much of it is simply disconnected bits of information? Consider where we get our news of the world. Most of it comes via television or the Internet. Less and less seems to come from books, newspapers, magazines, and other forms of printed media. This is because we as a nation are reading less in general.

The problem of getting news from watching television is that it is presented in a linear fashion. Stories of war and natural disaster are followed by summaries of medical advances, sound bites from politicians, or the activities of well-known people. It's difficult in this format to know what to attend to and what to ignore. Since 24-hour news channels have more time to fill than there is useful information to convey, we are bombarded with stories that might or might not be interesting but are seldom important: searches for missing white women, forest fires, "entertainment news" involving people better-looking than we are, some of whom are on trial for one crime or another. This is all "noise," distracting us from the "signal," that is, events worth noticing.

Then there is the large amount of airtime consumed by a small group of people who for no discernible reason have been selected to tell us what to think about this ocean of information in which we are swimming. These "analysts" and "experts" generally have a particular political or philosophical prism through which they view the events of the day. Often two or more of them representing opposing interpretations are speaking together (often simultaneously at high volume) in the interests of "balance," the assumption being that every issue has two sides and that by viewing both, the public is enabled make up their own minds. The problem with this is that some issues do not have two sides. For example, any debate that solicits the opinions of those who believe that it is acceptable to torture other human beings is not illuminating.

Our minds have a large but finite capacity. If we fill them with junk there is little room for anything important. It is also impossible to pay attention to more than one thing at a time. Whenever a survey is done about what people know, whether it is about geography, politics, mathematics, history, or current affairs, everyone is amazed at the apparent ignorance of their fellow citizens. Many people are clueless, for example, about the identities of their own senators and representatives; a majority do not recognize the Bill of Rights and often find its contents unacceptable; they cannot locate Iraq on a map; they do not know who fought in World War II.

If it is difficult to recognize what to pay attention to in the passing scene, how much harder, then, is it to integrate any of this information into useful knowledge? Knowledge requires the assimilation of information into a framework that promotes understanding. To do this we must be able to glimpse "the big picture" so we know where a particular fact fits. For example, if we are presented with photographs of prisoners being abused in Iraq, we can interpret this as an isolated departure from a military policy of humane treatment of detainees. Or, we can recall the atrocities previously perpetrated by occupying forces, including our own in

Vietnam, and conclude that such crimes are an inevitable and routine consequence of such wars.

One of the reasons that it is difficult to organize and understand the meaning of passing events is that there are inevitably people with access to the public megaphone who are eager to interpret facts to suit their own perspectives. We are exposed to this frequently in the legal system, where two opposing views of each case are presented to juries in the hope of influencing them to see defendants as responsible or not for what has happened. "Yes, she killed him, but he was abusing her." "As CEO he enriched himself, but he was totally unaware that anything illegal was happening." "Yes, his DNA was at the crime scene, but it was planted by the police." And so on.

Long experience has shown that when new information conflicts with our well-established preconceptions it is either ignored, denied, or interpreted in such a way that our worldview remains intact. If one believes in a certain political philosophy or religious doctrine (e.g., the inerrancy of the Bible), facts that conflict with such beliefs will be reinterpreted to fit them. And so, homosexuality, which is almost certainly an inborn trait, becomes "a lifestyle choice" subject to deprogramming. The existence of fossils that have been carbon-dated as millions of years old cannot be allowed to challenge the biblical account of a six-day creation occurring six thousand years ago. If committed to the fairness of the death penalty, no quantity of studies showing its lack of deterrent value or inequitable imposition will cause its advocates to reconsider. It turns out that most of what passes for knowledge is simply ossified prejudice in which facts are used to justify our core beliefs. If one has an investment in the idea that one's own nation or ethnic group is superior, no new information on the subject is likely to alter it. Our basic sense of ourselves will not permit us to believe otherwise.

The highest rung on the ladder of cognition, above both information and knowledge, is wisdom. This desirable attribute, presumably the result of considered thought and long experience, is remarkably hard to come by. We wish wisdom were an inevitable consequence of age, but the behavior of most of the elderly makes it clear that it is not. If we have never been able to refine and modify our views in response to new information, we are unlikely in our old age to acquire this habit or to have any better basis for what we "know" than when we were in our younger days. The hallmark of wisdom is to have distilled from one's experience some conception of how the world works that is useful to others. Such a capacity has some integrative and predictive value that enables us to look at novel situations and judge how they fit into some schema that enables us to make good choices. For example, certain behaviors have predictable consequences. If we can discern what these outcomes are and can transmit this knowledge to those caught up in the repetition compulsion that causes them to make the same mistakes over and over, then we are worth listening to.

It is a valuable journey, this ascent from collectors of information to purveyors of knowledge who hope to become wise. Even though none of us completes it, the effort to do so dignifies our existence as something more than the accumulation of material goods and the relentless pursuit of our own self-interest. And by making the effort we come a little closer to answering for ourselves the fundamental question of human existence: Why, after all, are we here?

Happiness requires an ability to tolerate uncertainty.

We all wish that life were simpler. Practically every unwanted emotion that we experience—fear, anxiety, depression, prejudice—reflects a reaction to the complexity by which we are surrounded. One way to deal with the confusion and messiness of everyday life is to adopt an absolutist worldview that admits of only two alternatives in any situation. We can conceptualize the world in terms of a struggle between good and evil, right and wrong, correct and faulty, us and them.

I remember my indoctrination into the Honor System at West Point. "Honor," we were told, "is like pregnancy: you either have it, or you don't." A cadet could not lie, cheat, or steal, nor tolerate those who do. What could be simpler or more satisfying than that? *Any* violation of the code resulted in dismissal; if you behaved dishonorably once, you were not fit to live among honorable men. The problem is, of course, that this is an impossible standard. How does one, for example, respond to the question, "Does this dress make me look fat?" The answer, "Yes, it does; you *are* fat," might be truthful, but it is not calculated to strengthen a marriage.

When I was at Fort Bragg in the early '60s we were visited by President Kennedy. Someone came up with the idea that the 82nd Airborne Division would assemble on the airfield, each battle group dressed for a different sort of combat environment. So we had some units in jungle fatigues, others in desert brown, and my own in all white with skis. There we were in the hot Carolina sun, many of the troops never having seen snow, posing as if prepared to fight in the Arctic. I remember thinking at the time that this was a lie directed at the president with more serious potential consequences than affirming falsely that one had shined his shoes that morning, an offense that had led to the dismissal of classmates from West Point.

The problem with inflexible moral verities and absolute

codes of conduct is that they are unattainable in the long run and therefore productive of guilt and a sense of having been compromised when we fail to meet their demands. They are, in short, invitations to hypocrisy. When a man of the cloth proves to be a sexual deviant, or when the author of a book of virtues turns out to be an inveterate gambler, or when a moralistic broadcaster is revealed to be a drug abuser, we are treated to the spectacle of people whose desire to sit in judgment of others has collided with their human frailty. It is a tribute to our public capacity for forbearance (or stupidity) that these people in general escape any real consequences of their hypocrisy and deceit and go on telling the rest of us how to live.

The practice of psychotherapy involves being willing to tolerate a high level of uncertainty (unless, of course, you are fortunate enough to do your work in public, in which case you are *never* unsure). The problems that people present to therapists are invariably difficult to understand and solve. If they were easy, patients would have already solved them. This is why good therapists are sparing with specific advice. This is not an act of modesty; it is an acknowledgment that other people are the best sources of solutions to their own predicaments. It is also a sign of confidence in people's ability, with a little help and active listening, to work things out themselves.

Another attribute that is often tested along with our tolerance of uncertainty is *resilience*. We all experience losses in life, especially as we get older. How we respond to these assaults on our sense of order and predictability determines our mood and ability to function. In other words, the attitude we take toward what happens (or what might happen) to us governs how we respond. Even life-threatening events produce different reactions, both short- and long-term, in different people. Not everyone exposed to combat, for example, suffers from post-traumatic stress disorder.

Once I evaluated a young man who had been a passenger in a car that had been pulled over by the police. According to an officer, the passenger had given him the truck driver's salute. The young man became belligerent and claimed that it was not illegal to display his middle finger to a police officer. Not surprisingly, he was arrested for disorderly conduct and spent a few hours in jail before charges were dropped and he was released. He promptly filed a lawsuit claiming, among other things, that he suffered post-traumatic stress disorder—with sleeplessness, depression, and flashbacks—as a result of the arrest. I suggested to him that the "trauma" he had experienced was, to a significant degree, self-inflicted and did not, in any event, rise to the level of the life-threatening stress usually associated with PTSD. Not surprisingly, he found another psychiatrist to testify on his behalf at trial. The jury found in his favor and awarded him $1 in damages—a decision, I thought, worthy of King Solomon.

Perhaps the most consequential (and most rewarding) occasion on which we must embrace uncertainty is our willingness to fall in love. Here is where our capacity for trust and commitment collides with our life experience, which is filled with examples of the evanescence of human attachment. A marriage proposal has been compared to stepping off a cliff in the dark in the expectation that a soft landing awaits. Life doesn't get more uncertain than that. And yet people line up to do it, on the promise and with the expectation that they will be winners. Perhaps it's the same impulse that fills the planes to Las Vegas. Our urge to gamble, often against prohibitive odds, is based on our need for excitement and the inexhaustible power of hope.

One of my favorite lines in a country song is "I wish I didn't know now what I didn't know then." Life is constantly surprising us, often unpleasantly. How we react to this atmosphere of uncertainty determines to a large extent how happy we are. Faced with death and taxes as our only guarantees, it's a wonder that we ever muster the courage to get out of bed, except that bedrooms turn out not to be such safe places, either. (How many hopeless mistakes have we made there?) Here comes the heavy hand of paradox again:

Those who are willing to improvise do better than those who imagine they are working from a script. Put another way, if we think of ourselves as (largely) the authors of our own life dramas, we are likely to enjoy the trip more than those who rely on others for instruction.

In fact, those among us who promote a simplified version of how to live tend to want everyone to adhere to their version of the rules. Unfortunately, life turns out to be complicated, at both its molecular and philosophical levels. Anyone who has studied biology and spent any time trying to decipher the Krebs cycle or the structure of DNA has to be impressed by the complexity of the chemical processes common to all living things. It is not a course of study for those seeking simple answers.

The same complexity dominates the science of human behavior and accounts for our difficulty in predicting how people will act in any given circumstance. Is it surprising, therefore, that our motivated behaviors and moral constructs would likewise be diverse and complicated? They are the "maps," after all, that we rely on for guidance. What is the likelihood that any one person or like-minded group would come up with the one true map, applicable to everyone, which, if followed, would allow us all to live in peace and contentment? Not likely.

So how do we reconcile all this diversity of belief and

difference of opinion on how to live? Whatever the answer to this question, I think the core value we need to cultivate is a willingness to accept behaviors in others that do not interfere with our ability to pursue our own happiness in the way that seems best to us.

As we grow old, the beauty steals inward.

We exist only to discover beauty; all else is a form of waiting.
—Kahlil Gibran

Apart from death itself, nothing terrifies us more than growing old. Our associations with advanced age—loss of physical attractiveness, increasing infirmity, decreasing independence, cognitive decline—all cause us to look with dread at the relentless evidence of aging. Even while relatively young, we examine ourselves for wrinkles, hair loss, weight gain. We spare no effort or expense to combat these physical depredations. Beyond the age of thirty, the greatest compliment any of us can receive is that we do not look as old as we are. It is further evidence, as if more were needed, that we live in a culture that values form over substance.

Given that most of us strive for longevity, it seems ironic that we so fear old age. Are there no compensations for our physical decline? An elderly patient of mine reports responding to a store clerk who brightly told her that she didn't look seventy-five by saying, "This is what seventy-five looks like." Why can't we all confront our aging bodies with similar equanimity?

We have created euphemisms to cushion the passage to senescence. The term "golden years" is the source of a good deal of black humor among the old, particularly as they experience the inevitable losses that come with advancing age. "Senior citizen" is likewise a patronizing designation that is devoid of reassurance and full of irony with its false connotation of increased status.

It is not hard to detect a certain mutual resentment between the generations. Jokes about the slowness and incompetence of the elderly, debates about when one is too old to drive, the tendency to marginalize and segregate people on the basis of age, all betray a reluctance on the part of the young to contemplate what they will inevitably become.

At the same time, the old are intolerant of the tastes and behavior of succeeding generations. They don't like their music, their clothes, or their lack of manners. There is, to be sure, an element of envy of the prerogatives of the young and regret at what has been lost. Who has not felt resentment toward those who have what we most long for? If what we lack is something we may later get, we can console ourselves with the virtue of patience. If, however, we envy youth when we are old, what hope is there for us?

Is there any compensation for the losses that are our lot as we grow older? Leisure time? *How to spend it?* Financial security? *To do what?* Relief from the burden of striving? *What relevance do we retain?*

The ultimate rebuke to our humanity at any age is to be ignored. Children know this. They would rather be punished than not noticed at all. To feel that no one is paying attention is a form of madness and is intolerable. Terrible crimes are committed by those who feel powerless and unnoticed. Yet it is precisely this feeling that is the lot of the aged. Bereft of a sense of purpose, denied the significance that society attaches to paid work, old people are frequently segregated into warehouses that offer only images of decline and death and where they feel utterly silenced.

Such attention as they do receive usually consists of grudging visits from family that are brief, infrequent, and weighted with obligation.

Where, then, is the beauty? Like all worthwhile human qualities—courage, kindness, determination, grace—beauty exists in the eyes of those trained to appreciate it. Because we live in a superficial world, the conventional view of what is beautiful in people is narrowly confined to the young. It is accepted that people who are attractive have an easier time in the world. Doors are opened for them, literally and figuratively, and they are often (incorrectly) assumed to have other qualities that we admire—intelligence and compassion, for example. Indeed, many actors in this select group whose images adorn our magazine covers are confused in the public mind with the characters they play.

Little wonder that these icons of our imaginations will do anything, including injecting themselves with toxins, to hold on to their youthful appearances; and it is unsurprising that we imitate their desperation. These are, of course, ultimately, losing battles, and time has its way with our bodies and minds. And yet there are compensations for growing older, if only we can appreciate them.

Erik Erikson, in his "Eight Stages of Psychosocial Development," designates the years after sixty-five as the stage of "Maturity." He suggests that the essential conflict in this period is "integrity vs. despair" and that the important task is "reflection on and acceptance of one's life and death." What is sought is some feeling of fulfillment and resolution with those we care about who will survive us.

What is absent from this formulation is any sense that creativity or energy can be a part of this stage. In fact, the conventional conception of these retirement years is one of leisure until physical or mental infirmity overtakes us and we are no longer able to indulge our pastimes. Nor is there much attention paid to whatever learning we are able to transmit to subsequent generations. Little wonder, then, that old people live up (or down) to the expectation that they have little to offer others and simply need to have as much "fun" as possible and then prepare to die. Where is the beauty in this?

I wonder if an alternative way of spending this stage of life might entail less golfing and more communication. Presumably, this would require some reflection about one's life and what it has meant, some self-forgiveness for mistakes and unfulfilled dreams, leading finally to a reconciliation with the past that would allow us to model for those we love the final and essential task of letting go of our earthly selves.

One mechanism for doing this that some families have used is the oral history. An elderly family member is interviewed at length about his or her life. All available memories are collected and recorded. The transcript is illustrated with old photographs, then bound and distributed throughout the family. The healing and illuminating power of this exercise cannot be surpassed. The person being interviewed is gratified that children and grandchildren are interested. It gives the old person a chance to reflect, to order, and to extract meaning from his or her life. And the resulting reminiscence can be a lasting bond between the generations.

One such history from a family friend ended as follows:

Somehow, in spite of my early failings as a father, the children have all turned out to be fine people. Successful, loving parents, every one, far better than I. They seem to be well situated in their lives and happy. We all get together for holidays and special occasions. Everyone gets along; it's just grand. I'm proud of my accomplishments and proud of my children and the lives they've made for themselves. I can say with deep satisfaction that I've led a full and rich life.

20

Every snowflake in an avalanche pleads not guilty.

I f each of our lives is meant to be an exercise in personal responsibility, what of our collective life as a nation? One would think from our recent behavior that we are a triumphalist people, frequently and publicly declaring America to be the keeper of the flame of freedom, the last best hope of mankind in the eternal struggle between the forces of good and evil. It pleases us to imagine that God smiles on us and all our works. He even supports our efforts to extend the blessings of freedom and democracy to the rest of the world, whether they want them or not.

There is no doubt that this country has been on the right side of many of the most challenging struggles of the last two centuries. Nor is there doubt that we have during that time perpetrated some grievous wrongs. In this way our national existence is a variant on the old good news/bad news dichotomy that is close to a defining rule in human affairs. We tolerated slavery in our founding document, then fought a bloody civil war that ended it. Still we live with its legacy. We pay homage to the rights of minorities even as we accept all sorts of discrimination. We defeated totalitarianism in World War II, yet have supported many similar regimes in the years that followed. And so on.

We know that we are not perfect, nor always correct in our disagreements with other nations, yet we are quick to denounce as unpatriotic those among us who point out the frequent contradictions between our ideals and our actions. We are, above all, fond of military solutions to problems. This is an extension of a philosophy that sees human beings as fundamentally flawed and who can be controlled in their base natures only by a threat of punishment. This idea is fundamental to the dominant religious belief that we were placed here by God to worship and to be tested.

We generally select for our leaders people who exude self-righteousness and pretend to have answers to problems like poverty, drug abuse, and national security—problems that seem to persist even after generations of voting for those who promised to solve them. What these leaders cannot do is save us from ourselves. Seldom does a politician say, "I don't have the answers to these intractable questions. I can only do what you will allow me to do." Nobody, apparently, wants to hear that.

And yet it is the truth. We are only as good or as smart or as powerful as our collective behavior entitles us to be. If we allow our leaders to send soldiers into foreign countries without sufficient reason (or worse, on the basis of lies and mistaken assumptions), should we be surprised when some of them engage in crimes of war? Can we absolve ourselves from responsibility by prosecuting a few miscreants in uniform? *Means are ends.* We cannot defeat evil by employing evil actions in the name of laudable goals. When we find ourselves arguing about what constitutes torture on the scale of mistreatment of other human beings, we have lost our way.

Why are we so resistant to this lesson? In our private lives we would not attempt to justify crime as a means of advancing our interests or our personal philosophy. We have, in fact, created an elaborate legal system to punish those who attempt to do so. Why wouldn't we expect our behavior as a nation to be held to similar standards?

Abraham Lincoln, at one of this country's most precarious moments, said, "Fellow citizens, we cannot escape history.

We . . . will be remembered in spite of ourselves. The fiery trial through which we pass will light us down, in honor or dishonor, to the latest generation." Note that he did not say "in victory or defeat." He said "in honor or dishonor." In the bloodiest conflict in this nation's history he was preoccupied with these values because he knew his Gospel: "What will it profit a man if he gains the whole world but loses his soul?"

To criticize this country when its (always temporary) leadership violates the core values of individual worth and human dignity is a profoundly patriotic act. Those who endorse the idea of "my country, right or wrong" are subversives who would use the flag to blindfold us all.

*Most people die with their music still
inside them.*

One of the signs you're growing older is that you start
reading obituaries of people you didn't know, especially the ones who are about your age. Like funeral eulogies,
obituaries tend to emphasize the positive aspects of the life
of the departed. This is natural; he's dead after all, why
bring up his alcoholism, his tendency toward infidelity, his
neglect of his children?

Perhaps it's because writing obituaries is not the most
coveted assignment at the newspaper, but there's not much

to be learned from them. This is too bad, because there is a potential for useful information here. Rather than the "puff pieces" that pass for summaries of people's lives, how much more interesting it would be if obituaries were written by the deceased. In fact, we might all do well to write one for ourselves, starting in our twenties, and revise it every year or two. What better way to confront who we are, what we're doing, what it all means, and whether we're making any progress toward becoming the people we would like to be remembered as?

I actually give obituary writing as an assignment to patients from time to time. Like constructing an epitaph, this can be an illuminating exercise. Just as with an obituary written by others, what we write about ourselves can be a work of fiction. But the process of selecting how we would wish to be remembered has a way of focusing attention on what we have done, or—more important—failed to do with our lives. The obituaries in the newspaper where I live typically identify people by their occupations—professor, restaurant manager, soil consultant, homemaker—as if that is how they ought to be remembered. It turns out, of course, that when people write their own obituaries, they are likely to identify themselves as parents, volunteers, or antique-car restorers.

People also tend to be more balanced about their lives

than the typical eulogizer. Those who have overcome addictions, for example, report this as a signal achievement. Mistakes they made as parents are frequently placed side by side with statements of love for and pride in their children. People are also pretty good at sharing what they have learned, often at great pain and expense, from their lives. The real power of the exercise, however, lies in the regret that most of us feel (and that is never mentioned in actual obituaries) about our unfulfilled dreams.

It turns out that few of us are living the lives we imagined for ourselves when we were young. We are often better off financially than we would have predicted, but it is unusual for someone to report that he is happier than he ever thought he would be. In fact, there is a kind of wistful quality among most people in middle age or older. This frequently takes the form of nostalgia for a simpler life that held more possibilities than the one we are actually living.

The advantage of writing one's own obituary is that there is still the possibility of changing and adding to it. Some people have provided a variation on this exercise by the use of what has become known as "ethical wills." Unlike a conventional will that is used to distribute money and property, an ethical will is a statement of values that one imagines might be of interest or guidance to those who survive us. Constructing such a testimonial seems like a good idea, whether in contemplation of imminent death or as a sort of midlife inventory of experience and beliefs that one would like to pass on to one's survivors.

The problem with the statements I have read is that they tend to contain a lot of advice. This is, I suppose, yet another example of the usual dialogue between the generations in which those who are older feel a need to tell those who are younger what to do. How much better received we would be if we simply told our stories and left the moral for our listeners to divine. In writers' workshops the operative instruction is "show, don't tell." This implies that we learn best about values by seeing how other people have expressed what they believed in by their actions and not by being told to "follow your passion," or "do unto others . . .," or "live an honest life." Most of us know what we should do; we just need models of how those who have gone before us have reified their beliefs.

It's not surprising that when we contemplate our mortality we tend to feel a little desperate about being remembered. "He not busy being born is busy dying," Bob Dylan said. *His* music will not be buried with him.

About the Author

GORDON LIVINGSTON, M.D., a graduate of West Point and the Johns Hopkins School of Medicine, has been a physician since 1967. He is a psychiatrist and writer who contributes frequently to *The Washington Post,* the *San Francisco Chronicle,* the *Baltimore Sun,* and *Reader's Digest.* Awarded the Bronze Star for valor in Vietnam, he is also the author of *Only Spring* and *Too Soon Old, Too Late Smart.* He lives and works in Columbia, Maryland.